# Woke-Free Church

*For the Deliverance of the Body of Christ
from Social Justice Captivity*

Jeff Kliewer

Unless otherwise noted, Scripture quotations are from the ESV Bible (The Holy Bible, English Standard Version), copyright 2001 by Crossway, a publishing ministry of Good News Publishers. Used by permission. All rights reserved.

Cover Design by Jennifer Kliewer

Editing by Rick Thompson

Copyright © 2021 Faith House Publishers

All rights reserved.

ISBN: 9798458095372

# RECOMMENDATION

Jeff Kliewer has written a concise, easy-to-understand volume that informs, equips, and challenges Christians to confront the social justice movement with biblical truth and a biblical understanding of justice. Jeff's insights are not theoretical but realistic and practical —- informed by more than a decade of ministry in the inner city and by careful study. Now an EFCA pastor, Jeff recognizes the forces at work in the evangelical world compelling church leaders and Christians to jump on the social justice bandwagon. Responding with a prophetic voice that is all too rare in the Christian community today, Pastor Kliewer warns that the social justice train isn't just going to a very undesirable place, it's also blinding its generally well-meaning passengers with a false and unbiblical perspective that makes them pawns of cultural Marxists intent on imposing their secular, statist religion on the general populace. Confronting and pushing back against these subversive efforts will not be easy, but reading this book will help you to be adequately informed, forewarned, and equipped. Don't miss a word!

--B. Nathaniel Sullivan, writer and founder
of wordfoundations.com and discoverbedrocktruth.org

# CONTENTS

# ACKNOWLEDGEMENTS

I am very grateful for all who fight against the intrusion of social justice into the Church. To those in the battle, it is my honor to be called your brother, fellow worker, and fellow soldier (Philippians 2:25). Special honor is due (Romans 13:7) my fellow elders of Cornerstone Church. Having prayed together and decided together to take up the fight for a woke-free EFCA, here we stand. We are blessed to have Cornerstone Church standing with us. I would also like to thank Voddie Baucham, J.D. Hall, James White, Samuel Sey, Jon Harris, A.D. Robles, Darrell Harrison, Virgil Walker, Michael O'Fallon, Cody Libolt, B. Nathaniel Sullivan, Jacob Brunton, and Tim Hurd. Their writings and podcasts on the subject of social justice have sharpened my thinking. I appreciate each of you very much. Please join with me in praying for the effect of this book upon the EFCA, and upon everyone who reads it. "Unless the Lord builds the house, those who build it labor in vain" (Psalm 127:1).

# INTRODUCTION

Bibles were not allowed in the Russian Gulag. If the guards discovered that Paul Kliewer was carrying one, then he would be punished severely, maybe even killed. Only one out of six who entered the Gulag would ever make it out alive.

As Paul neared a checkpoint, he had to think fast. The guards were searching the prisoners for contraband. They would surely check his coat and find the Bible. Just when all hope seemed lost, an idea suddenly flashed into his mind. He noticed that his water canteen was just larger than the size of his Bible. What's more, it had a large snap-down top, so that, when opened, there was enough room to squeeze the Bible inside. He decided to risk his life, pour out the water, and hide the Bible in the canteen.

At the checkpoint, the guards checked every pocket and even made Paul open his mouth to prove he wasn't stashing anything behind his teeth. They never thought to check the water canteen, probably because it seemed to be about the right weight and, they must have figured, no prisoner would dare waste their water ration to hide anything in there. By God's grace, Paul managed to keep his Bible with him in the Russian Gulag for all four years of his slavery.

On the train ride out of the USSR, on Paul's journey to freedom, propaganda officers tried to convert him to Marxism. They extolled the benefits of their society. "Equality," they said, was their highest value. "In the motherland, government cares for you. She would never let anyone starve. There are no homeless people. There are no greedy rich bankers living in palaces while working men are forced to beg at their gates." With grandiose language, the propagandists extolled the imagined virtues of Communism. Consider the hubris of these men to think that someone who just spent four years in the Gulag, watching five out of every six of his friends die along the way, would consider converting to the very thing that held him as a slave.

The Marxists confiscated Bibles because they understood their enemy. The Bible is the book that sets men free. On December 26, 1991, the USSR collapsed, largely because the most Christian nation on earth brought it to its knees. The USA won the Cold War because the truth sets men free, and free men cannot coexist with Marxism.

My grandfather, Paul Kliewer, lived to tell the story of his years in the Gulag. Had he not, my father, and then I, would never have been conceived. Wokesters would have no reason to be concerned about the content of this book. It would never have been written.

But the Marxists didn't give up when Stalinism failed and the USSR dissolved. They still kept believing even after Mao Zedong's "Great Leap Forward" resulted in 45 million people starving to death in China. They remained undeterred when the killing fields of Pol

Pot's Khmer Rouge in Cambodia were exposed to the world. Nothing could dissuade them from believing that "equality" must be elevated to a position as Chief Among the Virtues. The Marxist adoration of the goddess Equality wasn't born of any facts in the first place. So, no actual outcomes could ever change their minds. They always simply assume that their theory must be tried again, even if perhaps in a slightly different way.

What happened in Russia didn't stay in Russia. Sixty years after Paul was released from the Gulag, his grandson (yours truly), being newly married, moved into one of the poorest neighborhoods in the inner-city of Philadelphia. We were there as missionaries. Between 2004 and 2016, we would see more than 100 people enter the waters of baptism, proclaiming freedom in Christ.

Esther[1] was one of them, and her face was radiant the day she was baptized. To this day, I still remember the remarkable joy that shone on her face that day.

Since her home life was brutal, one of the other missionary families took her into their home. She would live with them for a number of years, right up until she left for college in North Carolina. What a story of deliverance her life was turning out to be.

But in college she started dating a guy who didn't believe the way the missionaries taught. Within a few years, she came around to seeing the world his way. In that world, the missionaries hadn't given their lives away to try to give to her and others an invaluable treasure (Matthew 13:44). They actually oppressed her. They exploited her in

---

[1] Some names are changed to protect privacy, but the stories are true.

order to profit off her story. By telling their financial backers about a poor girl who converted to Christianity, the missionaries could make a lot of money. Think of all the donations they receive. So, in the upside-down world (Isaiah 5:20) that this girl learned to envision while she was at college, missionaries were leaving the comforts of the places in which they were raised to live in America's version of a Gulag… in order to "get rich" on the backs of the poor.

As she continued down that philosophical path, our little Esther, like a star falling from the sky, eventually departed from the Faith. She renounced Christianity. Propagandists, like the ones who failed to convince Paul Kliewer, who had seen the final destination of the Marxist train, convinced Esther on a college campus in the United States of America that the poor are poor because the rich are oppressing them. Esther became a prisoner in the woke Gulag.

Quintin had a sharp mind. He had a quick whit and made people laugh. He and I were on the same team when we divided the basketball players from Teen Club into squads and formed a "Basketball and Prayer" league. While two teams at a time faced each other on the court, which was the church's sanctuary with all the chairs stacked to the side and portable hoops rolled into place, all the other teams met in another room for a prayer meeting. Quintin was happy in either station. He was a point guard on the court, and he was always one of the first to lead out in the prayer room. He and I had a special connection. I had hoped he would grow up to become a pastor one day.

Instead he encountered a new form of teaching. Friends of his convinced him that the "whiteness" of all the missionaries meant something more than how much melanin God chose to put in our skin. The missionaries who told him about Jesus weren't actually sent by God. They were colonizers sent by white devils. They were oppressors advancing a European white-man's religion. Quintin would one day side with these friends. He renounced Christianity and said the Shahada, becoming a Muslim and another prisoner in the woke Gulag.

Over the years, I watched Esther's story and Quintin's story play out in at least twenty lives. Jessica had sexual desires for other women. When social justice warriors pointed out that it was only the heterosexual missionaries telling her that her desires were wrong, she eventually left the Faith, concluding that homosexual desire is part of who she is and saying otherwise is oppressive. Sharon departed the Faith on the mantra "my body, my choice." "Who do these missionaries think they are telling women what to do with their bodies? How oppressive."

Time and again, people we thought were saved and who went down under the waters of baptism, departed the Faith to live as prisoners in the woke Gulag.

What does it mean to be free? For a prisoner or slave, it is to be chain-free. For an addict, it is to be drug-free. For a nation taken over by communism, it is to be dictator-free. For churches in this social justice era, it is to be woke-free. Here's to a woke-free Church.[2]

---

[2] For those connected to the EFCA, an extended introduction is in the Appendix.

*Woke-Free Church* was born out of my 12 years in inner city Philadelphia (2004-2016). In the early 2000's, Eric Mason graduated from Dallas Theological Seminary and set up shop in Philadelphia. His theology and experience led him to write *Woke Church* in 2018. I also graduated from Dallas Theological Seminary in the early 2000's and also set up shop in Philadelphia. We were about 3 miles away from Mason, but we were worlds apart theologically. By God's providence, my theological training and inner-city experience put me in a unique position to address the errors of the CRT movement. *Woke-Free Church* is the antidote to the poison of Mason's *Woke Church*.

I saw first hand that so-called "social justice" is rhetoric that enslaves, like so much of the language of the left. A group called *The Simple Way*, led by Shane Claiborne, was active where I lived in inner-city Philadelphia while I was there. They were SJWs before most of us had ever heard of such a thing.[3] Comparing what they said in the name of God with the Word of God (Acts 17:11),[4] it became apparent to me that what they were teaching was heretical.

In 2009, I visited a church in Florida and preached a sermon entitled "The Serpent's Cunning" from 2 Corinthians 11:3 to expose the lies they were bringing into evangelicalism. When a liberal worship leader at this church got up in the middle of my sermon and walked out, I knew I had touched a nerve.

---

[3] Ron Sider and Tony Campolo were forerunners of this movement, and like Claiborne and Mason, both were based in Philadelphia, the birthplace of this nation's Constitution, a city that needs to be set free all over again.

[4] I learned this expression "comparing what is said in the name of God with the Word of God" by hearing it often repeated by J.D. Hall on The Polemics Report.

It turns out that the nervous system of the social-justice-preaching left has nerve endings that reach far beyond the streets of the inner city. I've been carefully watching the leftward drift in American culture, with a particular focus on evangelicalism, since before 2009, and it blows my mind that Claiborne's views have become mainstream and even predominant in recent years.

I'm now five years into pastoring a church in the suburbs outside of Philadelphia. I'm far enough removed from the city to see my time there through a broader lens. But I'm near enough in time to remember what I saw when my boots were on the hallowed ground of the left. I've been to the final destination of their social justice train, and what I saw there resembles a Gulag. A large-scale acceptance of Marxism is what made the inner-city what it is.

In 2016, by grace, I began to pastor my current church. It is located in one of the most liberal states in the union—New Jersey, so I still see the devastating effects of wokeism all around me. But even so, by God's grace, the church is growing by leaps and bounds. People are hungry for truth. We've planted a second church and we're working behind the scenes to help faithful churches in the Philadelphia area carry out the Great Commission. We thank God for gospel advance (Philippians 1:12), but the biggest ideological enemy we're having to overcome, both here and in the city, is social justice.

I hate that the Church in America has generally been losing ground for over a decade. It really disturbs me that many Christians continue to say, "what's the big deal about social justice?". The sad reality is that many of the people who say that will one day find out how big of a deal it really is when young people they taught depart from the Faith. The head-in-the-sand Christians will often hold on to their Christianity, but those who follow rarely do. We're going to have to win this Cold War with this new form of Marxism, or we're going to keep losing disciples to it.

Leftist values prove too corrosive over time. For example, sending young men and young women to a university in America without equipping them with critical awareness to these issues is like dropping them in the ocean without a boat and hoping they'll swim home for Thanksgiving break. Parents must not abandon their children to deal with these issues alone.

*Woke-Free Church* is a book about Critical Social Justice, written to pastors, but in language accessible to all Christians. Academicians have for decades discussed the theory in the halls of the university, but in recent years what began as theory has reached the streets. Critical Social Justice is affecting very practical matters of life, from pop culture to conservatives being fired from their jobs for saying absolutely benign things. Meanwhile, the language that the left employs is brilliant in its simplicity and deceptiveness. Most of the people who espouse Critical Social Justice have no idea that they are under its influence. But let the reader understand.

So, we'll begin in Chapter 1 with the language of social justice. Let's get some cards on the table before we begin to explain how this game is being played. Chapter 2 is my attempt to establish ethos. Readers are right to expect to know why they should listen to me. What makes me a credible voice? Chapters 3 to 5 are the meat of my argument. Then chapters 6-10 are where it really gets interesting. I've been doing some traveling, sitting down with pastors who don't quite know where to land on this issue. These chapters address the objections I've heard from them. These five chapters are where the rubber meets the road.

We've heard the rhetoric of the noisy social justice warriors, but let every true pastor keep listening for the cross-examination (Proverbs 18:17). In conclusion, we'll see that every pastor needs to lead his people to be a woke-free church. And every Christian must speak out boldly against "social justice." As John MacArthur says, "Justice doesn't need an adjective."

# CHAPTER 1

## DEFINITIONS

In his poem, "On Hegel," dedicated to the predecessor of his thought, Karl Marx revealed why he never started with definitions. He wanted to string as many people along for as long as possible. Clarity, which is ever the friend of truth, was always Marx's enemy.

> "Words I teach all mixed up into a devilish muddle, Thus, anyone may think just what he chooses to think; Never, at least, is he hemmed in by strict limitations. Bubbling out of the flood, plummeting down from the cliff, So are his Beloved's words and thoughts that the Poet devises; *He* understands what he thinks, freely invents what he feels. Thus, each may for himself suck wisdom's nourishing nectar; Now you know all, since I've said plenty of nothing to you!"[5]

Marx meant to obfuscate, but what did Michael Rice, an EFCA pastor discussed in the extended introduction (see Appendix on page

---

[5] https://www.marxists.org/archive/marx/works/1837-pre/verse/verse15.htm

151), mean by employing terms like "hateful, systemic, trauma, racism, sexism, victims, and powerless"? Maybe he meant nothing Marxist, something completely different than what's being said at Berkley and Harvard. I hope so, but language of oppression bubbled out and plummeted down to the Eastern District pastors, whom I suspect weren't quite sure what he meant. It is critical for every Christian to gain awareness of where the language of oppression is coming from.

You'll hear me throw around the term "Critical Race Theory," or "woke" as a colloquial shorthand for the same. Wait for Chapter 8 to get in the weeds on the specifics of what I mean by that, but here at the outset, speaking of definitions, we need to note that a majority of Americans passionately support the fundamental tenets of Critical Theory without really understanding what they so confidently affirm[6] (1 Timothy 1:7).

That is owed to the fact that there is a group of leftist academics and elites that *do* understand Critical Theory as such, and although they are probably only 5% of the movement,[7] they, being highly motivated and extremely clever, have manipulated a majority of Americans to join their cause.

The intelligentsia of CRT are untethered by biblical notions of right and wrong. Defining terms and preferring clarity over

---

[6] Now that "Critical Race Theory" is common parlance and largely despised by conservative people, it is common for woke people to distance themselves from it. But believing in "systemic racism" or "white privilege", for example, without fulfilling the burden of proof to show that those things exist, is evidence of CRT, whether or not someone accepts the label.

[7] In one of James Lindsay's many presentations on CRT (I forget which one), he estimates that the intelligentsia make up only about 5% of the movement.

agreement are not universal values. The woke intelligentsia is willing to camouflage their ideas, dressing them up in deceptive language in order to win popular approval. Terms that used to mean something benign have become their vehicles to carry their theory.

The rhetoric they have introduced has changed the meaning of words like "left," "justice," "diversity," "inclusion," and "equity." The movers and shakers behind the scenes of pop culture know that many Americans will be willing to parrot language that sounds appealing. It seems they're banking on the old adage that "a lie can make it half way around the world before truth can put its shoes on."

They also know that when emotional stories are wed to fine-sounding terms, heat is introduced to the equation. Stories involving a victim are particularly emotional, because these stir the pious instincts of God's image bearers. Wherever we see victimization, God has wired us to not just look away. We're wired to hate it and to fight it.

Once we begin to fight for justice, whether or not questions of truth have been answered first, we have a tendency to keep on fighting. That's the God-given purpose of anger. The fire in the belly that motivates us to fight the wicked is only meant to die down when the war has been won.

When America saw George Floyd's face pinned to asphalt, we were furious. We were ready to fight. Enter stage left the fine sounding phrase "Black Lives Matter." "Of course they do!" answered America. "Black lives matter the way all lives matter!" And the innocuous-sounding phrase, which was actually introduced more than seven years earlier, surged forward on a wave of emotion.

But "All Lives Matter" was not what the ones who coined the phrase "Black Lives Matter" meant by stringing those three words together. In due time, those who coined the phrase would demand of it the meaning they invested in it. But the many people whose emotions compelled them to parrot the phrase "Black Lives Matter" would have to walk back their emotion-driven support, or else just keep on fighting, seeing this thing through, even though they had not done the necessary truth work at the outset.

As it turned out, in this emotional situation, far more people just kept on fighting their justice war. It seemed too late to go back and fight a truth war. So BLM won a nation. What never would have garnered much support if submitted the way theories ought to be, on the table and open for dispassionate evaluation and the test of time, suddenly became settled orthodoxy. Transparency at the outset would not have worked, but the way of deceit seems to have worked, probably beyond their own wildest expectations.

The left has a theory that they have introduced into the national conversation by way of deception. They snuck their ideas into the national psyche. And when we take a look under the hood, we'll see that the Critical Theory behind what contemporary society calls "social justice" does more than describe the way things supposedly are. It seeks to tear down Western civilization, especially Biblical Christianity.

When Critical Theorists teach people to say X, they mean for us to think X as we support the Y they actually mean. It is a system of lies. It is a clever use of language. Many Christians are all too happy to parrot the language of the left without knowing what is really being said.

It is critical for Christians to become aware of Critical Theory and wake up to the dangers of being "woke." If our children are going to be exposed to American culture at all, their lives depend on being aware of the snares that lay hidden under the brush of fine-sounding language (Colossians 2:4). Like good Bereans (Acts 17:11), let's prime the pump of this conversation by examining some of the language of Critical Theory and how the left invests terminology with new meaning in order to further their agenda. Here are ten examples of how Critical Theory deceitfully twists the generally understood meaning of words in order to tear down Western culture and the Church.

First, the CRT usage of "hateful" doesn't mean a spiteful attitude in the heart. Michael Rice says homosexuals view evangelicals as "hateful," but the critic doesn't know the heart of the accused. Hate used to be tied to the intent of a person's heart. But the vague accusation of being "hateful" is a misuse of the term. More than that, I have often asked such pastors to provide examples of Christians actually acting in ways that give external evidence of the Christian being "hateful" to gays. I haven't heard many examples. That's not to say there are no Christians who struggle with hatred toward gays. It is to say that the trope is a rhetorical device used to shame Christians into changing things that ought not be changed.

Second, the CRT usage of "systemic" doesn't mean actual laws or institutions. When Michael Rice used the term in our EFCA training, he offered no examples comparable to forcing someone of a certain skin color to sit in the back of the bus. Rather, "systemic" just means that there's a lot of it. It's not systemic as the word was formerly used, but "systemic" in the sense of supposedly being ubiquitous among people of low melanin, that is, "white oppressors." That's the real charge being leveled under the guise of "systemic racism."

Third, the CRT usage of "trauma, racism, sexism, victims, and powerless" and other similar terms that refer to *oppression* do not refer to *provable* sins or crimes. For example, Michael Rice named all 5 of the above buzz words without citing names or examples. There is an entire industry built around non-falsifiable grievance. Kyle J. Howard is a "racial trauma counselor." But don't be fooled. Unless the government passes hate-crime legislation and with it institutes thought-crime police, there will never be any investigation of what caused this so-called trauma. That's because these words do not refer to crimes or sins as we used to understand them. Rather, what's in view are so-called "micro-aggressions." It is enough if someone *feels* themselves to be oppressed for the new usage of the terms to hold.

Fourth, the CRT usage of "the city" isn't merely a population center. Tim Keller presents "A Theology of Cities"[8] that grants them

---

[8]https://www.cru.org/content/dam/cru/legacy/2012/02/A_Theology_of_Cities.pdf

an inordinate level of esteem. "City" doesn't just refer to a place anymore. "City" glows with a mystical aura of God's special affection. But cities actually aren't places of God's special affection. Where you have population density, there totally depraved people are concentrated, and there you will find a multiplication of wickedness.[9] The people of cities should be valued and we ought to bring the gospel to them, but glorifying cities is part and parcel of leftism. Keller thinks we should "recognize how much the city brings the gospel to us." But the old meaning of the term "city" did not include any notion of an inherent righteousness, let alone a righteousness it can impute to Christians.

Fifth, the CRT usage of "the left" isn't merely a perspective. Trevin Wax of The Gospel Coalition says "There's danger to your right, not just your left." He presents populist alt-right movements as if they were a parallel threat to what we're facing with leftism.[10] But "the left" ought not be viewed as merely having bad ideas akin to anything we're seeing on the right. Leftism is a singularly destructive

---

[9] "Harvey Cox attained international fame with the 1965 publication of his book *The Secular City*, which welcomed some aspects of secularization and critiqued the constraints of organized religion, even urging the faithful to find holiness in the world outside the church. Technological development, Cox argued, would bring about a kind of maturation in human development that would leave behind the age of the tribe and town and usher in a bold new secular and multicultural era. Christianity would serve a crucial purpose in the face of this radical transformation of collective human life by providing moral and spiritual support in these fast-paced, modernizing times. But it would also, Cox insisted, need to be reevaluated and retrofitted to survive society's increasingly secular, cosmopolitan sensibilities. *The Secular City* was spectacularly successful, selling nearly a million copies. Even Cox was surprised by its success." https://www.thenation.com/article/archive/a-moral-bulwark/

[10] https://www.thegospelcoalition.org/blogs/trevin-wax/theres-danger-right-not-just-left/

force. It is an absolute departure from the fixed landmark of the Bible on all issues. As Dennis Prager, widely acclaimed talk show host, often repeats, "The left ruins everything it touches."[11] We'll establish the weight of the danger in chapter 3, because so much of the error of those who make some room for CRT is a lack of discernment (Isaiah 27:11, Hebrews 5:14). Thinking of the "left" as a mere point along the spectrum of what's acceptable fails to appropriately weigh the proportions of what we're up against.

Sixth, the CRT call for "social justice" isn't for biblical justice. Thaddeus Williams of Biola University tries to strike a conciliatory note when dealing with social justice. He proposes that there is a "social justice A" that's good, whereas the extremes of "social justice B" are the problem.[12] But even 50 years ago famed economist Friedrich Hayak could see how dangerous "social justice" actually is. He rightly said, "I have come to feel strongly that the greatest service I can still render to my fellow men would be that I could make the speakers and writers among them thoroughly ashamed ever again to employ the term 'social justice'." The term "social justice" refers to something specific,[13] something that ought never to be granted even one iota of legitimacy.

---

[11] https://assets.ctfassets.net/qnesrjodfi80/61vbmLSohBfCuCW8B9hjBf/ef2303d b6c30604ebe0b815b0f259c70/Prager-The_Left_Ruins_Everything-Transcript.pdf

[12] https://www.amazon.com/Confronting-Injustice-without-Compromising-Truth/dp/0310119480

[13] I mentioned in the Introduction that Voddie Baucham's sermon "Defining Social Justice" is a helpful starting point for making sure author and reader are understanding terms the same way. Throughout this book, I'll be operating from Voddie's definition of social justice. "Defining Social Justice" by Voddie Baucham, https://www.youtube.com/watch?v=YFNOP2IqwoY

Seventh, the CRT desire for "redistribution" isn't for Christian charity. John M. Perkins wrote the forward to *Woke Church* and is celebrated by liberals and conservatives alike, but his three R's, "relocation, reconciliation, and redistribution," are a set of bad ideas. It's better to encourage movement away from cities, to declare the finished work of Christ in breaking down dividing walls of hostility, and to encourage private charity according to individual conscience. "Redistribution" implies there is a hand besides the invisible one of God and the invisible one of the market (supply and demand) to determine who gets what. Such a term is decidedly unhelpful and it derails the conversation, so people fail to see the Marxist underbelly of those who employ the term.

Eighth, the CRT usage of "diversity" isn't for anything colorful. Greg Strand picked a pastor to speak because in the EFCA there are "few who look like [him]." But such a narrow view of "diversity" actually diminishes how colorful[14] all individuals actually are. There are no literal doppelgangers. Even biological twins have differences too. So, being that people differ by height, weight, hair, nose, nose hair, and a thousand other variables, diversity is a given. The

---

[14] "Colorful" or "people of color" is a particularly wicked choice of terms. "People of color" set over against "white" people doesn't pass the scientific test of a kindergarten color wheel. "White" as a color is when no colors on the wheel are being filtered out. White is thus the definition of color. Conversely, black is when all color is being filtered out. Melanin filters out the reflection of light from the skin. When the sun's light bounces off a person of lighter skin tone, more of the sun's light is reflected therefrom. Darker skin reflects less. Although a few people on earth come somewhat close to being 100% white or black, almost everyone is far closer to the middle. Speaking in purely scientific terms, not according to the made-up language of leftism, it's racist to prefer "people of color," because that is to prefer "white" people, which is, ironically, the opposite of what they actually seek. The folly of the left is evident in everything it says.

consideration of how truly varied people are is how we arrive at individualism. But when the left clamors for "diversity," they actually mean less "white" people.

Ninth, the CRT usage of "inclusion" isn't kindness. Adolf Hitler was among the least kind people who ever lived. Would it be kind to include someone like him? Likewise, we would hope to exclude a spike under the tires, a sharp stick in the eye, a blunt-force trauma to the head, and such things. People who steal your money through Marxist redistribution schemes, backed by the threat of a government prison, people who seek to mutilate children suffering from gender dysphoria, people who love to murder babies, and other such people ought to be excluded. But the left speaks of "inclusion" as if it were a value in itself.

Tenth, the CRT usage of "equity" isn't equality. The clamor to make things equitable is a desire for Communism. Either individuals earn what they get by self-interested hard and smart work (2 Thessalonians 3) or there must be another entity that distributes to them. But distributing always requires taking from another to grant it, because goods and services don't just exist on their own without work. The word "equity" means the opposite of free markets and meritocracy. By it, the leftist means bigger and bigger government.

Critical Theory doesn't tear stuff down by calling itself "destructive." It calls itself "progressive," which, like most of its language, signals the exact opposite of what it actually is. "The city" actually means the Babel-like gravitation of sinners to one another for synergies of human depravity. "Left" actually means the enemy of all that is right. "Social justice" actually means the antisocial behaviors of injustice. "Progressive" actually means the falling away (the "apostasia" of 2 Thessalonians 2:3) of a culture from its nearest point to biblical fidelity.

We could go on and on examining the language of the left. We started to do so because defining our terms is where arguments ought to begin. Our goal here is to help the cause of truth hurry up and get its shoes on. Hopefully the reader is starting to get the gist of where I'm coming from and where I'm going. But before we go there, before we get into the meat of my argument, why should the reader listen to me?

# CHAPTER 2

## MY STORY

Oh how CRT loves its stories. When postmodernists jettisoned objective truth, stories were all they had left. So they got good at telling them, maybe to the point where they assumed they were the only ones with stories to tell. When Voddie Baucham or Candice Owens or Shelby Steele or Clarence Thomas or Thomas Sowell or Ben Carson or Virgil Walker or Greg Morse or Darrell Harrison or Larry Elder or anyone else with the requisite level of melanin tells their stories, leftists must just plug their ears. To my chagrin, at least they can point to the color of my skin as good reason to ignore mine.

Who are you to talk like this? It's actually a fair question. Appealing to skin color would be a terrible answer, but writers on any given subject really ought to be forced to establish ethos. Aristotle commended it along with pathos and logos.

For starters, my credentials include a Masters Degree from Dallas Theological Seminary, ordination with the Evangelical Free Church of America, and 21 years in full-time ministry. During those years, by grace, I've always seen the churches where I've served grow three dimensionally—larger in number, deeper in the Word, and outward in the relationships of believers one to another. I'm currently a Senior Pastor of a church in New Jersey that's growing quickly in these ways. To God be the glory.

In God's providence (little did I know He was preparing me for such a time as this), I majored in Economics in college. Social justice is cultural Marxism, and I have devoted a great deal of time to studying the spectrum of economic thought, from Marxism to Capitalism.[15] We even had a "History of Economic Thought" class at Eckerd College in which all the students role-played different economic philosophers. I was Thorstein Veblen for an entire semester. In order to pretend to level the charge of "conspicuous consumption" in my role as Veblen, I had to learn what the Marxists were saying. My best friend played Adam Smith, and I learned in college why his arguments were right. Through the writings of Wayne Grudem,[16] the Economics major from Harvard who is now a renowned theologian, I learned why capitalism is biblical and Marxism is an assault on biblical morality.

But I also have what I think is an interesting personal background that helps me understand issues of Critical Social Justice. If my parents hadn't taught me the biblical worldview, I would

---

[15] After college, I continued an informal study of Economics, learning a great deal from Ayn Rand, the Austrian School, Milton Friedman, The Chicago School, and members of the Hoover Institute at Stanford University, including Thomas Sowell, Victor Davis Hanson, and Shelby Steele.

[16] Wayne Grudem, The Poverty of Nations: A Sustainable Solution; Wayne Grudem, Politics According To The Bible; Wayne Grudem, Christian Ethics

probably believe in Critical Social Justice. Given the way I'm wired, I'm pretty sure I would be a full-fledged social justice warrior.

I was born and raised in postmodern America, grew up in Seattle and Tampa, went to public schools and a secular liberal arts college, and married a girl from New Jersey...not exactly a formula for conservatism. When Linked-In recently suggested I become a "Diversity-Inclusion Officer" at a public library, in a life without the Bible, I might have applied for it, instead of laughing myself right out of my seat. The only thing that has kept me all these years from becoming a SJW is knowledge of the truth as revealed in the Bible— the book that made me wise unto salvation (2 Timothy 3:15).

The Bible protected my wife as well. She easily could have fallen for the social justice siren calls of the Wesley Fellowship when she was a student at Duke University. That group talked more about Latin American politics than about the Bible. Having been taught the Word as a teenager, she could tell something was off with the Wesley Fellowship. At that time, social justice wasn't "a thing" that Christians generally understood, but something smelled funny when Honduras and Venezuela kept coming up every week at the Bible Study but the Bible was rarely opened. She separated from that group before it was too late. So, the Bible, and the Bible alone, kept both of us from becoming SJWs.

But even as committed Christians who understood something was amiss out there to the left of us, we were still somewhat susceptible to social justicey thinking. Many so-called "conservative" and "evangelical" churches are prone to unwittingly embrace unbiblical leftist doctrines, and we were prone to the same. From 2004-2016, when I was 26-38 years old, my wife and I were still pretty ripe for the picking.

In 2004, we got married and made our home in one of the poorest neighborhoods in America. We were missionaries. We were trying to make a difference. And we were as naive as could be. We didn't know the true reasons for the poverty, crime, violence, failing education systems, and deplorable conditions of the inner city. We didn't have Tim Keller's language of "doing justice" for the poor (an errant concept we'll address in Chapter 7). Nor did we assume victimization at every point. But because we were not entirely immune to social justicey thinking, and because we didn't always rightly answer the relevant truth questions first, a few of the decisions we made as missionaries were misguided.

Before becoming missionaries, we should have more clearly understood the true reasons for the condition of the city. But sadly, in today's PC evangelical culture, seminaries and missions agencies don't teach these things. In fact, the longer they exist, the further left those institutions tend to drift.

Nevertheless, despite having a highly naive assessment of the reasons for the problems of the city, and despite having a less-than-adequate anthropology, for the most part we stayed focused on offering to the people of the city the true and lasting solution to problems—Christ and Him crucified. 1 Corinthians 2:2 kept us where we needed to be. We offered the gospel for 12 difficult years, but we also had much to learn along the way.

We bought a row house (14 feet wide, 50 feet deep) for $27,000. That made for a $375 monthly mortgage payment once taxes and insurance were factored in. So far, so good.

But sharing walls on both sides meant sharing roaches, mice, and rats. Not so good. When the neighbor behind us kept throwing dead mice in plastic ShopRite bags on the roof of our kitchen, which extended out from the rear of our house, we were perplexed.

"Why is he doing that?" One of the things that makes inner-city America confusing is that answers to questions like that sometimes never come. Pat answers won't do. After a couple years of this, the man committed suicide. We'll never know what was going on inside of his head. Was he the victim of someone else? Or was he the oppressor? Was he "the marginalized" that we hear social justicians[17] talk about? Or was he the offender? Was he "sinner" or was he "sufferer" in the grand oppressor/victim meta-narrative? Maybe he was all of the above. But questions like that would have to be answered before any of us would be in any kind of position to offer a solution to whatever was going wrong.

One night in our Kensington neighborhood of Philadelphia, a teenager stole our credit cards and our car the same night we fed him a spaghetti dinner in our house. It was the night before his trial for another crime. When we weren't looking, he lifted our car key and credit cards. And that night, after saying thank you and goodbye, he was off with our car, joyriding with his friends. When we found the

---

[17] Phil Johnson of Grace To You coined this term in 2019. It rightly implies that there are many who make a trade out of what has become a grievance industry.

car and called the police and they arrived to help us get our car back, he disappeared into a house.

It's hard to say why he stole from us. But the "social justice" narrative is often set in the city. And applying the oppressor/victim construct would require answering truth questions before the crusade against victimization could ever justly begin. So, who is the victim in my story?

As my story goes, the young man showed up to his trial the next morning. When he saw us come in as he awaited his trial in the courtroom, he got up to leave. Another case was underway. But his grandmother interrupted the court proceeding to plead with the judge to arrest her grandson to prevent him from running, and probably winding up dead one day if he continued on the path on which he was headed.

When the bailiff grabbed him, the judge ordered him to be searched. To gasps from all the people in the courtroom, the bailiff read the names on the credit cards in the young man's pocket. When he read our names, I came up to get back our cards and car key, which was also still in his pocket. It was a very dramatic scene, looked like something out of a movie, but that is exactly what happened.

We made some unwise social justicey decisions in our dealings with this young man. After all that, we bailed him out of jail. We believed his stories. It seemed to us that the deck was stacked against him. Society was not built for his flourishing. He was a suffering victim as much as a responsible sinner. Our thinking was that he was a good kid that had been dealt a bad hand. So we did things like bail him out of jail.

Our anthropology was deficient at that point, because we should have considered more deeply that *no one is good* (Romans 3:12). Our offer of grace was cheapened by our failure to more clearly expose him to the Law of God. We offered cheap grace when he needed to be held accountable to God (Romans 3:19). Perhaps the mercy of the Gospel (Romans 3:21-26) would have fallen on him *after* feeling the weight of his sin.

The behavior of people in the city was not moral, and our response was not always wise. Social justice tells people they are victims. But the Gospel tells them they are responsible, then offers the gift of forgiveness.

I was the victim of the crimes of grand theft auto and credit card theft, but was I a victim of racism on a mission trip to the Bronx? Not long after the courtroom debacle, we took a number of teenagers from Kensington to the Bronx to run a Vacation Bible School for a partner church there. While the mission team was in the house (it was a row house like the ones we had in Kensington), some police officers saw me standing by myself on the corner, talking on my cell phone.

Not recognizing me, and suspecting that I might be trying to set up a drug corner, the cops circled the block and came up behind me. Before I knew it, they had pressed me up against a fence and were patting me down.[18] The police officers profiled me because I looked suspicious to them.

So, will the social justice warriors be consistent, on account of my story, and accuse the Bronx police of oppression, heterophobia, racism, misandrism, or anti-Americanism? After all, my story pits them against a middle-class, heterosexual, white, male citizen.

I didn't assume myself a victim. No, I thanked them for doing their job and told them I wished they were policing the corner where I lived in Philadelphia, since it had been an uninterrupted drug corner for the last six months.

The pursuit of truth would include being allowed to cross examine any charge, including charges of discrimination or the various –isms and –phobias. It wouldn't be right to make the charge unless the truthfulness of it could be established, allowing for due process. Since racism happens in the heart, it is always very difficult to prove that racism motivates the actions of police officers or anyone else. Being that I'm not a social justician, I don't assume that racism motivated those officers to stop and frisk me.

Returning now from the Bronx to Philadelphia, time and again, the scales of our naiveté were peeled from our eyes. A gang gathered to attack the teenagers from our ministry as they were leaving Teen Club. The gang appeared dozens of times over the course of a year. The leader of the group of attackers didn't look the part of a gang leader. Growing up, we thought he was a really good kid. We tried to teach him to read when he was young. For a time, he attended Teen Club. But a petty rivalry becomes dangerous when young men hit puberty. And 14-year-olds are more than capable of violent crime.

---

[18] This was before "Stop and Frisk" was outlawed in New York and murder rates shot back up.

This young man seemed to transform from saint to sinner as he grew up, and his story went from bad to worse. No need to recount it here but to say that our naive assessment that he was a good kid in tough circumstances was given the lie. He led a violent gang because the condition of his heart was just as Romans 1:18-3:20 describes, not because he was a good kid in a bad situation. He had opportunity to walk in the light that was given to him, but he hated and spurned that light (John 3:20).

Every year in Kensington brought multiple funerals for people we had grown to love, many of them children. A brother stabbed his own sibling to death. The one who died had been the life of the party at Teen Club. A twelve year old died of viral meningitis, perhaps contracted from unsanitary conditions. A girl was run over by a car. She was playing on the sidewalk and the car hopped the curb and took her out. The driver of that car was fleeing from the cops. These were all kids that we loved dearly, and it broke our hearts to bury them.

Sexual abuse was rampant in the city. Some say there are more people in the inner city who have been sexually abused than there are people who haven't been sexually abused. One young man we knew very well turned himself into authorities after confessing his ongoing sexual abuse of his young sister. Those occurrences devastated an already broken family.

While living in Kensington, it was not unusual for us to hear commotion and look outside to see some kind of altercation or brawl. One day I opened my front door to see one man pinning another to the ground and trying to get his wallet. After breaking up the mugging, the men pled their cases as to what was going on. Finally, after a minute of this absurd pleading, my wife appeared behind me and simply commanded the perpetrator to "go home." Surprisingly he obeyed. He left his poor victim alone and walked down the street with his head down. If only Beth Moore would obey John MacArthur's exhortation to "go home" the way this man obeyed my wife, perhaps the mugging of evangelicalism would come to a similarly peaceful conclusion.[19]

But during one half-year period, the perpetrators wouldn't go home. Drug dealers never left the corner in front of our house—Jasper and Orleans—for six solid months! Drug dealers were posted up, right in front of our house, day and night. It remained a drug corner until someone was shot and killed there (while we happened to be on vacation in Florida). At that time, the drug dealers set up shop on another corner.

Where Jasper Street dead ends into a fence that separates the street from an elementary school, drug users took advantage of the dead end, using it for a place to shoot up. It was also a common place for prostitution, since there weren't a lot of people passing by

---

[19] I know the risk of offending the tone police when employing strong language like this. However, I'm calculating that it is worth the risk because it helps draw attention to what matters. David Wood wins a thousand-fold more Muslims out of Islam and to Christianity than those who are more nuanced and politically correct. Social justice is a greater danger to the Church in America than Islam is. The culture is being swept away by social justice rhetoric, so strong language exposing the folly is appropriate (Galatians 5:12, Matthew 23). I know I am only a jar of clay (2 Corinthians 4:7-9), not in myself any better than the people I criticize, but the ideas of *Woke-Free Church* are better, and strong language is needed to combat the strong opponent of leftism (Matthew 12:29).

that way at night. We had thought that it would be a good idea to buy a house next to the elementary school because criminals might at least divert away from where children are.

The dead-end where the school stood created the opposite of our desired outcome. Whenever we wanted to take our daughter outside to play during the day, I had to first go through with gloves and put all the discarded needles in empty water bottles and trash them, so our daughter would have a semi-safe place to play outdoors.

But when night fell, terrible things happened there. One night, a taxi cab parked there to let the passenger out, but instead of paying and leaving, the passenger shot the driver in the head and took the driver's money. We watched from our daughter's bedroom window as the police and medics carried the dead body to the ambulance.

These are my stories, and they really happened. The truth they illustrate is that the devastation of the city is fundamentally a sin problem. The idea that the city is full of victims of society is absolute garbage. Sure, there are victims in all the crimes I mentioned. But those victims are suffering at the hands of sinners, not at the hands of society. Social justice assigns blame to the societal structures, such as laws, or such nebulous things as "implicit bias" and "white privilege." In truth, the blame lies at the feet of sinners, which all of us are, damnably so until God interposes on our behalf.

While social justicians decry disparities in racial representation in the prison population, a vast majority of individual prisoners are guilty of the crimes for which they are receiving punishment. The movie "Thirteenth," which is mostly social justice nonsense, rightly points out that 97% of prisoners have pled guilty to wind up where they are. So, if they were actually innocent, their own sin of lying is a big reason why they are behind bars.

Instead of arbitrarily assigning "race" to individuals, when we are all, in fact, descendants of Adam and therefore one race, instead of keeping track of prison population based on skin pigmentation, people should promote personal responsibility. Christians should issue God's command to repent and believe the good news (Mark 1:15). We may also advocate for righteous changes at the societal level, but in our activism, we must be sure to be on the side of the right.

There were great victories for the gospel during our years in the city. We saw over one hundred baptized. The church grew. A dozen or so teens made it to college, away from the city. During our years in Kensington, well over a thousand people filled out decision cards to indicate their decision to follow Christ. I don't think a great many of those decisions turned out to be genuine conversions, but some were.

I could go on and on about the experiences we had in the city, but it is not my intent to write a memoir. Rather, I share what I have because there are great lessons that apply to the content of this book. The problems of the city are not what the left claims. And the solutions are not what they prescribe.

Rather, it is social justice rhetoric that feeds the monster of sin in the city. And what happens in the city doesn't stay in the city. Social justice is threatening all of America and most of the world. The Church in particular is in its crosshairs.

We must first diagnose the problem before we can solve it. The Kensington neighborhood of inner-city Philadelphia is one of the poorest places in America. It is largely minorities who live there (ironically, having lived there, my family now knows what it is to live as a minority). Homosexuality and transgenderism are rampant there. There are lots of illegal immigrants. And there are more women than men. Kensington is hallowed ground to the left; The left has brought it into existence, and the left perpetuates it.

So, is the left's diagnosis of the problem truthful? Are homophobia, racism, misogyny, nationalism, and corporate greed oppressing people? Are the people of Kensington victims of an unjust society? Does that explain the poverty, filthiness, crime, violence, drug abuse, sexual abuse, and early deaths that run so disproportionately high in this place?

The story of my life, which includes 12 years devoted to the city, offers a resounding NO. Nothing could be further from the truth.

The truth is that the problems in Kensington are caused by sin. There has been an abject rejection of the Word of God by a vast majority of the people. We'll address the generational issues associated with the sins of the parents in chapter 9.

In his book Discrimination and Disparities, Thomas Sowell aptly traced out a high number of factors that must be considered before differences in outcome are diagnosed. That's the kind of work that truth warriors must do before ever becoming a justice warrior. Sadly, questions of truth don't often get answered before the justice warrior goes off fighting for a cause. But truth must always come before justice.

The root of the problem in the city is sin. I observed the variables play out in thousands of lives, and the primary difference between different people living in the same conditions in Kensington is the difference between sin and salvation.

Salvation, then, is the solution to the main problem. "Just preach the Gospel" misses the point that there are also societal changes that need to be made, made from left to right. But "preach the Gospel" is indeed the starting point of the solution to the problems of the city.

Salvation doesn't mean praying "the prayer" and being done with it. Salvation delivers individuals from the kingdom of darkness into God's marvelous light (1 Peter 2:9). Those who come to Christ will find Him to be a perfect Savior (Hebrews 7:25). Those who humbly submit to the teachings of the Bible will find the kind of prosperity predicted by Psalm 1. Husbands and wives will be of the Biblical kind (Ephesians 5:22-33). Fathers will be the kind of fathers that the Bible creates (Ephesians 6:4). Children will "obey [their] parents in the Lord" (6:1). What a different city that would make.

Social workers cannot solve the problems of the city. Their secular training doesn't equip them with the solution. Christians are equipped with the Gospel of Jesus Christ, powerful to change the hearts of sinners. Christians are equipped with the Bible, powerful to reorient individuals (and societies are made of individuals) to the thoughts, speech and actions that result in human flourishing.

In the language of the left, "the city" is a picture of human accomplishment. The magazine *Cosmopolitan* is nothing but immoral drivel, but such worldliness (cosmos is Greek for world) is the left's idealized vision of city life. It is a world without hierarchies, where everyone is equal, where people "own nothing but are happy."[20] Augustine had a vision of the City of God that stood in direct opposition to the city of man. The left envisions "the city" as a place of fun and freedom, like the man-made utopia of "Sex and the City," but "the city" isn't sexy.

Twelve years experience as a missionary in inner-city Philadelphia, wrestling with the harmful effects of Critical Social Justice, has earned me a hearing. We're all born with a right to speak, but ethos ought to be established in the minds of the listener based upon what the speaker has actually done. Greg Strand granted a special platform to one pastor because he had the experience of being a "POC." I denounce such standpoint epistemology. The content of one's character and what one has actually accomplished, not the color of one's skin, ought to be the basis upon which such assessments are made. What makes me an expert on social justice? Who am I to talk like this? I've studied this issue for 17 years, 12 of them with boots on the ground where social justice reigns ignominiously.

---

[20] In late 2020, The World Economic Forum presented their vision of the world of 2030 in these terms.

# CHAPTER 3

## WHY GO NUCLEAR

In August 2018, Dr. John MacArthur said, "Over the years, I've fought a number of polemical battles against ideas that threaten the gospel. This recent (and surprisingly sudden) detour in quest of 'social justice' is, I believe, the most subtle and dangerous threat so far." And that was two years before George Floyd.

If the reader wonders why I'm going nuclear against what seemed to be a relatively benign lecture given by Greg Strand and Michael Rice,[21] it's because I agree with MacArthur. On an impersonal level, this is the biggest threat we've faced in a generation.

On a personal level, I'm passionate because I've seen about two dozen of those inner-city Philly kids I mentored grow up and go

---

[21] The Extended Intro in the Appendix takes a teaching by Greg Strand and Michael Rice as a case study. If you haven't read that yet, turn to page 151. I'm not out for blood; I'm out for a seat at the table. I pray God uses *Woke-Free Church* for Greg and Michael's good. *Father God, please guard the hearts of Greg and Michael. Please draw near to them and grant them peace. Move in their hearts to receive what's being said. Don't let the enemy convince them they are personally being attacked. Let them reason objectively with regard to the ideas that are being presented to them (Isaiah 1:18). In Jesus' Name, Amen.*

apostate. More have remained faithful, but we've lost too many. All of them, similar to celebrities like Joshua Harris and Marty Sampson, did so on the wings of social justice. All of them were swept away by this subtle, evil, worldly current.

In that sense, social justice is a gospel issue. I have never seen anything comparable to it in its ability to draw away professing Christians. It should not surprise us. Where outright Communism took root, there was widespread apostasy. The USSR all but snuffed out the light of evangelical witness. Likewise, North Korea was once home to many Christians (Pyongyang was dubbed "the Jerusalem of the East"), but when a version of Communism overtook the country, the light of the gospel was all but extinguished. Today, there are more than 100 times more believers in Christ in South Korea (a free country) than there are in North Korea (a socialist country). So, if outright Communism has this deleterious effect on the progress of the gospel, then it should not surprise us that a cultural form of Marxism leads to apostasy. Of the couple dozen people that I have baptized that went on to apostatize at some point years down the line, every single one of them are presently spouting social justice rhetoric. Social justice is a gospel issue because social justice is our culture's strongest weapon against the gospel.

When I say such things, I am referring to secondary causes. There are real human wills that operate in this world. But the existence of instrumental causes, like these human wills, does not negate the existence of God's absolutely-free sovereign will. From the perspective of the Divine will (Ephesians 1:11), nothing is a threat to the gospel. We simply recognize that apostates go out from us *because* they were never of us (1 John 2:19). But from the perspective of the Christian in our war, we do not know the identity of the elect. Therefore, we must fight for souls. When someone is teetering on the edge of apostasy or has gone out, we contend for them (Jude 1:23). My fight against social justice is a fight for the Faith (1 Timothy 6:12, Jude 3-4).

McLean Bible Church, an evangelical mega-church just outside Washington D.C., has some woke pastors.[22] David Platt wasn't always one of them.[23] But since he began trying to lead his congregation to take on the cause of social justice, the church has seen a 40% drop in attendance.[24] Going woke has been like a straitjacket to David Platt and like a slave-chain to McLean Bible Church.

Before the 40% drop in attendance, we reached out to David. Back in 2019, a family who in the early 2000's attended Platt's church in Alabama moved to South Jersey and began attending our church—Cornerstone Church. They deeply respected David, because he had a

---

[22] On July 14, 2021, Pastor Mike Kelsey, a campus pastor of McLean Bible Church, was recorded saying, "Totally honest,…it is difficult for me sometimes not to just torch all white people…particularly white evangelicals and Christians."

[23] "As you look back on your time pastoring [at the Church at Brook Hills], before you stepped into the role at the International Mission Board (IMB), what's one thing, or a couple things, you would change?" Platt said, quoting his friend, "The first thing that came to my mind was . . . I look back, and I was not intentional about leading the church toward greater ethnic diversity, in a way that would be a reflection of the gospel in our midst," he answered." The Gospel Coalition, Why David Platt and Ligon Duncan Repented of Racial Blindness, https://www.thegospelcoalition.org/article/david-platt-ligon-duncan-racial-blindness/

[24] Capstonereport.com, June 9, 2021 "David Platt is harming McLean Bible Church with Woke Social Justice Theology"

profoundly positive influence on their family, even contributing to their decision to adopt a child from China. In 2019, when they began to see that David was moving into error, they wanted to help. Please understand, this family absolutely loves David Platt. To "love your neighbor as yourself" (Leviticus 19:18) is not incongruous with the verse that comes right before it; "you shall reason frankly with your neighbor" (Leviticus 19:17). According to Leviticus 19, reasoning frankly with a brother who has fallen into sin is a loving thing to do.

Since they knew people close to David Platt, and since I often raised concerns about social justice from the pulpit,[25] they decided to reach out to David. They asked for a meeting with him and myself to examine the Scriptures to see if his new-found woke teachings were so (Proverbs 18:17, Acts 17:11). Sadly, they were surprised to hear that their old pastor flatly refused the offer.

Our goal for the meeting had been to plead with David to avert the train wreck[26] we saw coming. Now it's here. McLean is in shambles. That said, it would be unjust for us to exonerate everyone at McLean Bible Church who opposed David Platt. We are not privy to all the facts, so it could well be that there was profound error on both sides of the divide. It would also be beyond the pale to claim that David Platt's wokeness is entirely responsible for breaking the church. There could have been other factors.

---

[25] Back in 2019, we produced a video called "Sweet Social Justice" (https://www.youtube.com/watch?v=HPM8d40wa3I) to plead with David Platt and others to abandon their new theology.

[26] The sermon "Train Wreck", May 2, 2021, pleads for woke pastors to repent (https://www.youtube.com/watch?v=FNMOA2AR4s8).

But consider what we were saying *before* the church suffered. Our criticisms were not ad hominem. We objected to David's handling of Amos 5 in his MLK50 sermon.[27] In that sermon, David criticized the conference for being too white, and he cited disparities of outcome as evidence of racism. Reasoning like that, through a social justice lens, is bound to be destructive. Going to a Christianized version of a BLM rally, alongside Mike Kelsey, while they had McLean Bible Church shut down for COVID was another outrageous example. And we objected to the book he released in the lead-up to the 2020 election. *Before You Vote* made room for voting for pro-death candidates. Teachers of God's Word are held to a higher standard (James 3:1). Since David leads many sheep, for their sake, we have spoken directly about David's teachings, and we attempted to sit down with him. It truly breaks our hearts that our brother is caught in such a straitjacket that he can't open the door to let us in.[28]

I'm sick of seeing social justice hurt the sheep.[29] I'll bring out all of my weapons to stop this from happening to young believers in the church I pastor now. I'm also willing to fight for the readers of this book whose faces I may never see.

In August 2020, being riled up against the enemy, like I am right now, I ruffled some feathers when I posted on Facebook that

---

[27] https://t4g.org/resources/david-platt/let-justice-roll-like-waters-racism-need-repentance/

[28] Father God, in the name of Jesus, we intercede for David Platt. Please bring him back to sober reasoning.

[29] John Piper's former church Bethlehem Baptist blew up in a similar way to Platt's church during the summer of 2021 after Jason Myer taught social justice. https://soundcloud.com/the-christian-worldview/tcwst-20200615-2-jason-meyer-evangelicals

"There's no such thing as a 'left-leaning Christian.'" I was attempting to show both the spiritual and the political dangers of social justice. The reaction to this post was strong, in equal and opposite directions. Christians "liked and shared" it in ways typically reserved for delicious-looking food, happy-go-lucky news, or cute pictures of kids or puppies. The left commented under my post with weeping and gnashing of teeth. Here's what I wrote:

There's no such thing as a "left-leaning Christian." Christians, as opposed to the left, have an absolute standard. One can lean this way or that (like a reed in the wind) if there is no definitive word on which way is up. But a Christian stands under the authority of the Bible. When the Bible teaches that life begins at conception (Psalm 139), there is no option to "lean toward" allowing that life to be killed. When the Bible teaches that sex is for one man and one woman in marriage (Matthew 19:4-5), there is no "leaning toward" the idea that "love is love." When the Bible teaches that all people descend from Adam and Eve (Acts 17:26), there is no acceptable "lean" in the direction of racialized collectivism. When the Bible teaches private property rights (Exodus 20:17), there is no innocent "leftward lean" toward anti-capitalist Marxist economics. When the Bible teaches that Israel is the apple of God's eye (Zechariah 2:8), there is no "leaning in favor" of redistributing their land. Leaning this way and that is the bad posture and sad predicament of the rudderless left. "Left-leaning" and "right-leaning" is the language non-Christians use to identify their position. They can only locate themselves with reference to where masses of other waffling human beings happen to be for a moment. Christians have an objective moral standard, so Christians don't lean. We stand.

Why did such strong language need to be employed? It was necessary because "left" isn't a mere perspective as compared with the "right." Social justice issues such as abortion, sexual sin, collectivism, Marxism, and anti-Semitism are not mere trifles. We cannot address them playfully, like children opposing one another in symbiotic relationship on a see-saw. "Left" is a direction, as well as a position. It is a radical departure from the Christian ethical system upon which Western culture was built. The opposite of left isn't just right, but Christian.

Leftism is a fundamentally destructive worldview that arose in opposition to the way things were. There is a gun shop in New Jersey called "Way It Was Sporting Services." I can imagine how the owner of that shop decided upon that name. He's an older guy. The left would call him "Boomer." But he grew up in a different era. The men of his day were of the kind that were willing to cross an ocean, storm the beaches of Normandy, and overpower Adolf Hitler. The women were of a kind that could hold families and society together even when the men were off saving the world. But now he looks around and sees squirrelly men and unstable women crying about the very instruments that his generation employed in opposition to the Nazis. And he longs for the way it was.

Christianity provided the moral backbone for the way things were. Sure, there were still unchristian elements in society, and individuals were still sinners by nature and choice, but there were some agreed-upon standards. And those standards were not arbitrary.

The Bible provided the basis for ethics.[30] The Ten Commandments were displayed in courthouses, and more importantly, they were entrenched in the Western worldview. The first four commandments protected God's honor. The next six protected horizontal relationships. "Honor your father and mother" established hierarchies and protected the family. "Thou shalt not murder" protected the sanctity of life. "Thou shalt not commit adultery" protected marriage between one man and one woman. "Thou shalt not steal" established private property and laissez-fare capitalism. "Thou shalt not bear false witness" protected truth and objective reality. "Thou shalt not covet" protected purity of heart.

Listen, "the left" is no ordinary foe. If America was justified in using 2 nuclear bombs to secure V-J Day, then I'm going to use every polemical nuclear bomb at my disposal to win for the Lamb the reward of his suffering.

The "left" is the palatable name that haters of the Christian ethic were willing to take for themselves. To couch the discussion in terms of directions—right or left—is a very postmodern thing to do. If there is no absolute standard, then all that remains is relativity. They don't see their ideas as deviants from the way things were, not in the

---

[30] Wayne Grudem, Christian Ethics

sense of departing from any standard. They see themselves as being merely over here, while others are over there—left and right.

The terms "left" and "right" implicitly grant legitimacy to both. There's no moral flaw in merely looking at something from a different angle. In fact, hearing as many points of view as possible is generally a good thing. Multiple points of view based upon where a person is situated should help a group arrive at a more circumspect understanding of a thing. And that is how the "left" wants to be regarded. They call themselves "left" in order to offer their perspective.

But the left already assumes its own legitimacy and they don't stop when others cede them ground. Left is a direction, so they are always moving. After gaining legitimacy (tolerance), they seek to win the majority, because that is what democracy is all about. But after having a majority, the only thing remaining for them to seek is dominance, and then absolute hegemony. "Left" never stops. They are never satisfied.

The left thinks they are see-saw riding toward progress. They hold Hegel's philosophy, so they always oppose the status-quo thesis by offering an antithesis, in the hopes that the synthesis that will emerge from the struggle will be one step closer to utopia. Since progress is to be won this way, there is no end to how far left they pull.

Left is a direction. God established hierarchies of authority; Left is a direction away from God's ordering of things. God made human life in His image; Left is a direction away from the sanctity of life.

God set boundaries for sex; Left is a direction away from restraints on sex. God granted private property rights; Left is a direction away from ownership. God demands truthfulness; Left is a direction away from objectivity. God looks at the heart; Left is a direction away from God.

Recognize that social justice is a two-fold danger. There are gospel issues at play, and there are issues of human flourishing at play.

Of first importance, social justice is a spiritual danger. It is one of the strongest forces in the history of the world[31] in getting professing Christians to apostatize. What the Roman sword failed to do for the first 300 years of Church history (Tertullian said, "The blood of the martyrs is the seed of the Church"), social justice does all day long.

Convince a young "black" man that the "white" missionaries who led him to Christ were actually colonizers attempting to impose their dominant culture on him, and he will eventually leave the Faith. Convince a young woman experiencing sexual attraction to other women that the "heteronormative" biblical sexual ethic is oppressing her and is morally wrong to be so "exclusive," and before long she'll "liberate" herself. Convince the poor that Western capitalism is their oppressor, and "Western religion" will eventually be jettisoned. Social justice leads to apostasy.

---

[31] Dennis Prager has repeatedly demonstrated that leftism has shown itself to be the most dynamic religion of the last hundred years.

Second, social justice leads to devastating social and political outcomes. It leads to dead babies, broken families, soaring murder rates, high inflation, and negative outcomes in all areas of life.

The big deal about allowing some leftism into our churches is that it won't pacify anybody, and it won't promote unity. It will feed the monster of social justice and strengthen the next leftward pull. Victim mentality is like a train with many boxcars.[32] The Christian who jumps aboard the race-victim car may have no interest in pulling along the gender-victim car, the LGBTQ-victim car, the economic-victim car, the nationality-victim car, the environmental-victim car, or any other victim-rights agenda, but the cars of the social justice train are hitched together. Christians need to unhitch now, because there's a train wreck coming.[33] Social justice is an attack that warrants a nuclear response.

---

[32] Voddie Baucham, Youtube "Biblical Justice vs. Social Justice"
[33] "Train Wreck", sermon on Hebrews 10:26-31 on Cornerstone Church Youtube page https://m.youtube.com/watch?v=FNMOA2AR4s8

# CHAPTER 4

## SO-CALLED JUSTICE

At the outset of a Gospel Coalition Conference[34] panel in 2015, D.A. Carson prayed for wisdom. He asked God to help the speakers. He also begged God to correct them if what they said wasn't wise. That was a godly prayer.

Voddie Baucham sat next to Thabiti Anyabwile. The two said some very opposite things. Since then, the fault line has only intensified. God's answer to Carson's prayer will only come from the Bible.

Is social justice actually biblical? That is the key question, and pending a Proverbs 18:17-style rebuttal to Voddie Baucham's biblical applications, it seems pretty definitive that the answer is no. Social justice isn't biblical. I'll offer some more evidence to corroborate that position. The Bible opposes social justice.

---

[34] https://www.thegospelcoalition.org/conference_media/biblical-foundations-seeking-gods-justice-sinful-world/

"Social justice" is the banner of the left. Leftists know that if they offered a course on Critical Theory, no one would show up. So they take their message to the streets, and the populist flag they fly reads "social justice." These hallowed words are sometimes accompanied by the insignia of the clenched-fist, which has always been a symbol of Marxism. But "social justice" is the starting point of all leftist rhetoric. It's the phrase that's never far away from any leftist cause.

"Social justice" is an odd term. It's "social," so we know it deals with groups or societies, not just individuals. And it's concerned with "justice," so it seems to address questions of morality, fairness, righteousness, and the like. But what is meant by modifying the noun "justice" with the adjective "social"? It's not at all clear what would be meant by that. More is meant than merely *making society right*. Or if it is simply that, we still have to define what is right or "just" for a society.

Like wolves who devour sheep and cover themselves with sheep skin to look like something they are not (Matthew 7:15), social justicians are not as virtuous as they appear. They do a lot of claw-pointing, never shy about leveling accusations. This is how they signal their virtue. Their posture is always one of righteous indignation.

They signal their own virtue by condemning so-called violations of justice. But many of the things they condemn are often, in fact, just the ways things are. They rail against "injustice," but what they find themselves deriding is often just the way God made things to be. Thus, they themselves not only practice immorality, since God is the standard of morality, but they also "give approval to those who practice [immorality]" (Romans 1:32), all while parading themselves as defenders of virtue (John 7:24).

Let's examine the morality of social justice by assessing its positions on its five biggest concerns—sexuality, race, gender, nationality, and economics. In so doing, *immorality* will emerge as the defining characteristic of "social justice" (Jude 15).

First, social justice is an immoral approach to sexuality. The Bible clearly sets the parameters for sexual morality. Any sexual behavior outside the bond of marriage, which, by definition, is a covenant between one man and one woman, is immoral. These are the moral boundaries of the Father, Son, and Spirit (Leviticus 18, Matthew 5:17, 19:5, 1 Timothy 1:10, 4:1) regulating sexuality.

But social justice says, "Let us burst their bonds apart and cast away their cords from us" (Psalm 2:3). Heterosexuality is considered to be a privileged orientation that imposes an unwanted and oppressive standard upon a minority victim class who is differently oriented. Therefore, rejecting the moral lens given to us in the Bible and applying an immoral lens imposed by the feelings of mere people, social justice advocates (who now, ironically, make up the majority) enforce their newfangled code by labeling those of us who espouse biblical morality as homophobic, bigoted, intolerant, and hateful. Social justice is thus the virtue-signaling enforcement of immorality.

Second, social justice is an immoral approach to race. The Bible clearly describes humanity as one race descended from Adam and

Eve. Ethnicities are presented as mere geographic and cultural distinctions (Genesis 11) that are woven together in beautiful unity for those who enter the body of Christ (Ephesians 3, Revelation 7:9-10), where there is no "Greek and Jew, circumcised and uncircumcised, barbarian, Scythian, slave, free; but Christ is all, and in all" (Colossians 3:11). Identity is to be found "in Christ," as that phrase is employed 75 times in the New Testament. Thus, biblical morality views humankind as one race and Christ as the destroyer of every dividing wall of separation. Christ has done the work! Our part is to be thankful and walk in the freedom He has already won for us.

But social justice rejects creationism and Christianity, opting for the evolutionary model whereby different "races" do not share a common ancestor. It necessarily follows that some people are more evolved than others. They create a construct whereby some humans are "people of color," whereas others are "white." Even leftist creationists accept this narrative, not by the evolutionary model, but by adopting Critical Race Theory that ascribes "whiteness" to whoever it is that supposedly has power or privilege. Whether stemming from an evolutionary worldview or not, to categorize people as "people of color" or "white" is a deceitful artificial binary.

A moral view would consider the spectrum of difference between the amount of melanin in peoples' skin as a mere trifle—literally only skin deep—based upon micro-evolutionary adjustment to exposure to the sun (depending on nearness to the equator) and make no substantive distinctions thereby. But the social justician immorally categorizes people by melanin and, unjustly, even slanderously, accuses the "white" of racism against "people of color," not based upon any actual mistreatment or hatred in the heart, but based upon supposed "white privilege" and "implicit bias." Social justice is thus the virtue-signaling enforcement of immorality.

Third, social justice is an immoral approach to gender. Jesus, whom the social justicians would like to claim is on their side, referencing Genesis 2:21-25, asked, "Have you not read that he who created them from the beginning made them male and female...?" (Matthew 19:4). Gender, according to Jesus, is therefore not a spectrum, but a binary. God makes every individual to be one or the other, never one trapped inside the body of the other.

But the immoral social justicians would even shatter this bond, committed as they are to absolute human autonomy. God must not be allowed to determine gender. This must be a free-will choice of the almighty humans, each one a little god. They would go so far as to tell children who struggle with gender dysphoria that the problem is their body. Horrifically, they would take it further still, prescribing medications and even performing surgeries that mutilate the very body that God created. This is an unspeakable immorality.

The abortionists are equally immoral in their quest to make women the same as men. Snuffing out the life of pre-born children so as not to inconvenience women who, unlike men, sometimes get pregnant, is the ultimate picture of immorality pursuing equality. But social justice presents transgenderism, feminism, and abortionism as righteous crusades against misogyny, sexism, transphobia, hate speech, and toxic masculinity. Social justice is thus the virtue-signaling enforcement of immorality.

Fourth, social justice is an immoral approach to nationality. Job 12:23 teaches us the truth that it is God who "makes nations rise and then fall." Both Peter (1 Peter 2:13-17) and Paul (Romans 13:1-7) teach the morality of remaining in subjection to the authority of the nation under whose governance you are situated, unless that nation has laws that force disobedience to the higher laws of God (Acts 5:29, Hebrews 10:25). You are born into a particular country according to God's providence (Acts 17:26). When seeking to immigrate from one nation to another, the moral thing to do is to abide by the laws that govern that migration.

But social justice religion assumes that people must be more autonomous than that. Their immoral view of reality does not allow government to be any kind of determining factor in life. Therefore, to build walls, whether they be physical or not, and to enforce national boundaries is called immoral and xenophobic. Social justice is thus the virtue-signaling enforcement of immorality.

Fifth, social justice is an immoral approach to economics. The Bible teaches that it is God who makes men to differ in terms of wealth. God made Job exceedingly wealthy and Lazarus exceedingly poor (Luke 16:19-31) in this life, and God has His own good purposes for every financial circumstance He ordains for His people (Philippians 4:11-13). God has a secret will. Moreover, He has a prescriptive will that morally governs our choices. "You shall not covet your neighbor's house...wife...anything that is your neighbors" (Exodus 20:17). Private property rights are moral, and the moral heart does not covet.

But social justice rejects private property rights in favor of Marxist redistribution schemes. The very foundation of Marxism is envy. Coveting (Exodus 20:17) the "exorbitant wealth" of "the 1%" or lamenting the unequal outcomes that free enterprise and private property necessarily entail, the social justician decries "capitalistic greed," "economic injustice," and "income inequality," and violently wields the sword of government (that is supposed to punish wrongdoers) to confiscate wealth (via unnecessary and excessive taxation) for distribution according to its own political determinations. Social justice is thus the virtue-signaling enforcement of immorality.

The immorality of social justice is seen in everything it touches. Whether it be power grabs or money grabs hidden under the cloak of environmental protection, like the Green New Deal, the five examples provided above, or practically any other pet cause that the social justician takes up, it is immorality masquerading as justice. Again, as MacArthur says, "justice doesn't need an adjective." The insertion of the word "social" is the tell that something other than justice is being promoted.

That is because social justice is fundamentally a Marxist modification of justice. True justice, plain-old justice, is defined by the Bible. For example, not showing favoritism to the rich *or to the poor* is justice (Exodus 23:3). But social justice proposes "God's preferential option for the poor" (Gustavo Gutierrez). God doesn't actually prefer the poor. We know that from the Bible. Consider Job, Abraham, David, Solomon, Paul at times (Philippians 4:11), Jesus at times (Matthew 2:11), the Saints who belonged to Caesar's household (Philippians 4:22), and the rich/poor division of heaven and hell that will characterize the eternal state.

Although cloaked in fine sounding arguments (Colossians 2:4), social justice is simply immorality. Wherever you see lies signaling their virtue, wherever you see immorality in a fit of rage against what is actually moral, wherever you see justice perverted yet claiming the moral high ground, you have identified social justice.

The Moral Majority was an ill-fated conservative political movement of the 1980s and beyond. It sought to marshal the resources of typically silent, not-so-politically-minded "moral" people across America. Mostly churchgoing folk, these Americans had offered little resistance during the 70's when the political left brought moral travesties like Roe vs. Wade upon the country. Jerry Falwell and other prominent evangelicals rallied the troops, together with like-minded non-Christians, in the late 70's and early 80's to stand up to the leftist juggernaut that was destroying the moral fabric of America. Although valiant in many regards, the movement eventually discovered that they were not the majority. Sadly, neither were they moral.

Unless a person is genuinely born again and thus has the righteousness of Christ imputed to him, he is not moral. Even if a lot of its people go to church, a political action group comprised of both saved and unsaved people ought never be described as "moral." It may champion some moral causes. For example, Ben Shapiro is an unsaved Jewish conservative who has been like a wrecking ball to the deceitful political ideologies of the left, but lacking regeneration, he is also prone to grave error, such as when he opined in favor of mandatory COVID vaccinations.[35] But the moral sword of truth only fits in the hand of a righteous person. When immoral people take it up, it turns on them and exposes their hypocrisy. The Moral Majority was destined to fail because it was neither moral nor a majority.

Social justice is stronger than The Moral Majority ever could have been. It will probably continue to expand until Jesus returns, because it has already become a majority. But let me be clear: Social justice is *The Immoral Majority*.

---

[35] https://nationalfile.com/conservative-ben-shapiro-makes-the-case-for-mandatory-vaccinations/

# CHAPTER 5

## MARXISM

Marxism is satanic. You can feel the breath of the enemy on the back of your neck when you listen to the words of Karl Marx.

> "With disdain I will throw my gauntlet full in the face of the world, and see the collapse of this pygmy giant whose fall will not stifle my ardour. Then will I wander godlike and victorious through the ruins of the world and, giving my words an active force, I will feel equal to the Creator."[36]

Satan was the power behind the king of Babylon (Isaiah 14) and the king of Tyre (Ezekiel 28), and in the same way, he empowered Marx. Marxism appears to be Satan's most recent attempt to establish himself as god. In that sense, Satanism and Marxism are one and the same, where the former is the in-your-face version and the latter is the under-the-radar version, masquerading as "justice." Most

---

[36] Menschenstolz by Karl Marx https://www.jstor.org/stable/25600101?seq=1

Americans rejected Marxism at first, but recently the allurement has been increasing.

If you told Americans in 1971 that 50 years later Christianity would no longer be the majority religion in America, they would have laughed at you. If you told most Americans today that Christianity has already been replaced by a new majority religion, they would scratch their heads. They would be highly skeptical, thinking about the relative obscurity of Islam, Buddhism, Hinduism, Mormonism, Jehovah's Witnesses, Scientology, and what not. Almost nobody would recognize Marxism as a religion. But it is, and it has grown silently to majority status while everyone thought its adherents were merely secular.

One would think that the deep (and profoundly good) roots of individualism in American society would have left little room for Marxism to be accepted on American soil. But Marxism found in "social justice" a more innocuous sounding term. "Social justice" is an expansion of Marxist economics, expansive in that the fundamental Marxist worldview of oppressor/victim Conflict Theory is spread out across the expanse of sexuality, gender, race, nationality, environment, and any other area where outcomes are never equal. Social justice is a broadening out of the Marxist economic concern. In that way, social justice and Marxism are practically synonymous. They are everything America isn't, or at least everything America was intended by its founders not to be.

Social justice is essentially a Marxist political cult. Advancing leftist political power is its great commission. Social justice activism gives the adherent a sense of meaning in life. It begins with a "born-again" experience of conversion, going from asleep to "woke." And it highly prizes zeal. The more zealous the better. For some adherents, this religion has as much single-minded devotion as the followers of Jim Jones displayed when they drank the cool-aid. It promises a utopia once the dark forces of racism, sexism, homophobia, transphobia, bigotry, and the like have been overcome. It has a priesthood, imputing special knowledge, even gnostic secrets, to people who have hallowed identities. It has sacred books, like Robin DeAngelo's *White Fragility* and Jemar Tisby's *The Color of Compromise*. It banishes those who transgress the faith.[37]

In the next chapter, we'll address the decline of Christianity, because that is what left the vacuum for social justice to occupy, but we must first consider from whence this fundamentally religious social justice movement came. It was sired by a Marxist father, born of a Catholic mother, and is being kept alive by postmodern doctors.

The father of social justice is Karl Marx. Marx lived during the Industrial Revolution. Being a rather pessimistic soul, he began to lament the economic disparities that seemed only to intensify as capitalism did its thing and, lacking the benefit of time to see how the Industrial Revolution would play out, he undervalued the benefits. He didn't live to see that in the last 200 years industrialized capitalism has done more to help the poor than all other helps put together. What caught Marx's myopic eye was that under capitalism, outcomes were *unequal*.

---

[37] The 2019 Social Justice and The Gospel Conference at G3 in Atlanta,, GA was where I first heard of social justice bearing all the marks of a religion.

Marx theorized that the bourgeoisie rich were getting rich by oppressing the proletariat poor. That is to say, the poor were poor because they were being victimized by the rich.

Marxism is an oppressor/victim lens for viewing reality that calls for a revolutionary overturning of the social order to make things just. It is the foundation of social justice ideology.

Marx is the father of social justice, but the Roman Catholic Church is the sweet mother. During the 1830's, swooning under the influence of Marx's writings, the Jesuit philosopher and popular author Luigi Taparelli began to sing a similar tune. Enamored with Marxism, yet devoutly Roman Catholic, Luigi Taparelli found a way to marry the two. He was the first to use the term "social justice." Ironically, it is a religious term that religious people made popular.

What was first called social justice became a large part of official Catholic Social Teaching once Taparelli popularized it and convinced the Pope to accept it. From there, it crossed the Atlantic Ocean to Latin America where it found very fertile soil in which to take root. Social justice wooed hearts from Venezuela to Colombia to Cuba. Liberation Theology developed Catholic Social Teaching through the writings and influence of Gustavo Gutierrez.

Socialism surged south of the border of the United States of America. But until the late 1960's, it made little headway in the land of the free and the home of the brave. In the early 1900's, a Protestant counterpart to Roman Catholic Taparelli, a theologian named Walter Rauschenbusch, began to echo the term "social justice," but his "social gospel" made little progress after the First Word War.

But if the American people before 1970 weren't having it, that didn't mean that the intellectuals weren't enamored. And so, when the hippies of the 60's grew up to become the professors of today, social justice made some inroads along with them. Social justice entered the mainstream of American life through the universities. Graduates of these universities have gained significant footing in media, government, education, sports, and virtually every aspect of American society. Social justice, the child of Karl Marx and the Roman Catholic Church, is coming of age in the United States of America.

Social justice arose by the illicit relations of Marxist philosophy and Roman Catholic theology, but it took more than that for social justice to survive in America. Social justice couldn't have made it here had it not been for postmodern midwives such as Duke University's Jacques Derrida. Postmodernism is the intellectual virus that constantly tries to kill truth. Wherever the Correspondence View of Truth is affirmed—and not only as a subjective affirmation but as an absolute certainty—postmodernism tries to deconstruct it.

Social justice would have died an ignominious death by now were it not for the weakening of the American understanding of truth. Absolute truth destroys socialism faster than chlorine kills viruses. So, credit Derrida and the postmodernists for so watering down the American conception of truth that abject lies can be treated as subjectively-valid privatized "truth."

"Who are you to say that social justice is unjust?" asks the postmodernist who has been conditioned to believe that nothing is absolutely right or wrong, except the absolute wrongness of affirming absolutes. By convincing the world that the only thing intolerable is intolerance, postmodernists have disarmed the critical minds of Americans who, until the 1960's, would have looked at raw facts and found them incompatible with the way social justice claims things to be. If Americans held a Correspondence View of Truth, then reality would be obliterating social justice.

When social justicians claimed systemic racism, the fact that the laws of this nation are not racist would have mattered to the discussion. The fact that there has never been shown any evidence of racism in Derek Chauvin's killing of George Floyd would matter. But postmodernism allowed *the feeling* that significant systemic racism exists to be enough to establish the truthfulness of the claim for the one who makes it. Likewise, the woman who feels oppressed by American systems, the LGBTQ+ person who feels like a victim of society, or the illegal immigrant who feels oppressed by the society he illegally entered, are all considered truthful *merely because* they *feel* the way they do. Everyone has "my truth" to tell, and no one is allowed to falsify anybody else's "truth."

That's how social justice grew up in America despite the fact that every major claim it makes today is overwhelmingly contradicted by all objective evidence. Karl Marx fathered a theory with a Roman woman. They named their baby social justice. It grew easily in Latin America, Russia, China, north Vietnam, and certain parts of Europe.

But it took the breakdown of truth in America to give it a chance to live here.

Biblical Christianity is entirely resistant to social justice. But the father of social justice—Karl Marx—wasn't a biblical Christian. In fact, he started from at least two patently unbiblical and decidedly wrong assumptions.

First, Marx assumed that people were morally neutral. Given more equal opportunity, the world would be a better place for all. In truth, people are morally bankrupt (Romans 3:23), and the power brokers who must necessarily distribute resources within a non-capitalistic system will default toward their evil nature. Unless there were born-again, mature, Spirit-filled, wise leaders at the top of the system (and there couldn't be since such leaders are made by the Bible, which fundamentally opposes non-capitalistic systems), the system would become more oppressive than anything it sought to correct. Marx didn't account for the true condition of man, a condition that makes figures like Stalin, Hitler, Mao, Castro, and Pol Pot not only likely but necessary, apart from God's restraint.

The second wrong assumption that undergirds Marxism is the idea that the earth naturally provides for the needs of people. Marxism insists that everyone *deserves* such *rights* as food, clean water, shelter, clothes, health care, education, transportation, communication devices, etc. because "just look at how much stuff there is!". Surely with so many resources all around us, they ought to be distributed equally, or at least equitably enough to provide for basic human needs.

The truth is that the earth is a killer, and hostile to humanity. Lions left to their nature—untamed and uncaged—will kill you if you meet them on the plains. Diseases are bent to destroy and adapt themselves to overcome the cures we develop against them. Harvests don't abound naturally, but only abound to those who till and seed and water and weed and *work* to collect the harvest. All the stuff that abounds is the result of human work. It is not naturally there. Wealth must be brought up from a hostile earth through hard and smart work. Without work, there is nothing to distribute (2 Thessalonians 3).

Marxism fails because it doesn't understand the world or those who live in it. But it found a lover in the harlot of Rome who claims to be Christian but doesn't understand the Word or what is written in it. She espoused him because she herself had long since departed from truth. And America only received her illegitimate child—social justice—when the foundations of truth were sufficiently undermined by postmodern philosophy.

Only a postmodern could look back on socialism's track record over the last hundred years and conclude that it ought to be tried again. Social justice is only thriving in America because there is so little truth to kill it. That's the story of the rise of social justice in America.

Now to the five biggest objections I've heard to what I'm saying. I've been listening even more (James 1:19) than I've been talking (and my church will tell you I've talked a lot about this). From Greg Strand's presentation to private conversations in the offices of fellow

EFCA and non-EFCA pastors, I've heard five major protestations: 1) But Christian nationalism is just as dangerous, 2) But don't name names or throw fellow Christians under the bus, 3) But we haven't studied CRT, so we aren't into it, 4) But broad and obvious disparities must be caused by racism, even if it's hard to prove individual cases of it, and 5) But now you're getting too political. We'll address these five objections in chapters 6-10.

# CHAPTER 6

# CHRISTIAN NATIONALISM

*"But Christian nationalism is just as dangerous"*

Greg Strand actually had two presentations the day he addressed the EFCA East pastors about these issues. The first 1.5 hours were meant to decry Critical Race Theory, although, as I have said, the last half hour of that was commandeered for quite the opposite purpose. But the second 1.5 hours were meant to decry "Christian nationalism," and we heard it often repeated that this, not Critical Race Theory, is the major danger we are facing.[38]

In his presentation, Strand called Mike Pence to the carpet for admonishing his audience to "fix our eyes on Old Glory." The

---

[38] It would be helpful to listen to Strand's Christian nationalism presentation before reading this chapter, because this chapter begins with an interaction with that material. Enough context is provided here that the reader will be able to follow without first listening to Strand's presentation, but more will be gained if taken the other way around. Greg Strand, Contemporary Critical Theory: A Biblically-grounded and Gospel-guided Response, EDA Theology Refresher, March 11, 2021, https://vimeo.com/user71521019

patriotic sentiment made allusion to Hebrews 12:1-2, where Jesus is the one in view. Strand may be right that Pence overstepped his bounds and failed to recognize the sacred nature of the actual words of the text to which he was alluding. Trying to make anything in any way equivalent to the Name that is above every name is a fool's errand. It's probably not what Pence meant to do, but in any case, score one for Strand for pointing out the irreverence.

Yet Strand goes on to complain that Pence's language and similar language promoting Christian nationalism "can begin to sound almost exceptionalism." That's a wider criticism.[39] Is "exceptionalism" something to be derided?

American exceptionalism is a term that came into vogue following an 1831 visit of Alexis de Tocqueville and Gustave de Beaumont to America. They were ostensibly sent by the French government to study the American prison system, but Alexis de Tocqueville indicates that they were really there to study American society. His assessment was very positive, and one of his observations may have given birth to the phrase "American exceptionalism": "The position of the Americans is therefore quite exceptional, and it may be believed that no democratic people will ever be placed in a similar one."

David Barton offers a definition of "American exceptionalism" that many, if not most, evangelical Christians would affirm.

---

[39] Opposition to "nationalism" is a rising phenomenon in our culture today. Bill Rhoden of ESPN says, "Nationalism is not good," and he laments that he cannot enjoy the opening ceremony of the Olympics anymore, ever since he saw American flags waved on January 6th. The world is making "nationalism" a boogey man.

"American exceptionalism is the unprecedented stability, prosperity and liberty that has resulted from institutions and policies that were produced by a unique set of ideas and philosophy."[40]

American exceptionalism says that the Mayflower Compact explains to some measure the exceptional fruit born of American soil. Those aboard the *Mayflower* sailed "for the glory of God and the advancement of the Christian faith." Building from the foundation of biblical ethics, to a degree never before seen in world history, the results speak for themselves. But Strand, like Prince Humperdinck of the Princess Bride, seems to warn Barton, "I would not say such things if I were you." It is verboten to call America an "exceptional" nation.

In his presentation, Greg Strand called out men like Eric Metaxas and Mike Pence, and perhaps hinted at others like Barton, but he cited as helpful a handful of others. He did not give unqualified approval, but choosing them for a reason, he took as positive contributors to this conversation Mark Dever, Karl Trueman, David French, Robert Benay, Jonathan Leeman, Paul Miller, Andrew Whitehead, Samuel Perry, Tim Keller, and Scottie Smith.[41] Let's take a moment to find out where a few of these men stand.

---

[40] David Barton, https://www.youtube.com/watch?v=IAFhb82eTPo

[41] For example, in his presentation Strand says, "Mark Dever says in his book "God and politics; David French was asked about this "resist the language of existential physical threat"; Robert Benay has spelled this out; Jonathan Leeman talked about this at our theological conference last year, "most issues are jagged line issues", "none of us should claim to possess the Christian position"; Paul Miller serves with the ERLC and is writing a book with IVP on Christian nationalism. "CN is the belief that the Christian nation...prescriptive program for what America

Can we figure out where Mark Dever stands? At ShepCon 2019, a kerfuffle between Phil Johnson and John MacArthur on one side and Mark Dever and Al Mohler on the other exposed how deeply divided American evangelicalism really is.[42] Mohler became visibly angry and defensive, while Dever positioned himself as coolly indignant and offensive. Dever (and Mohler, for that matter) are clearly left of Johnson and MacArthur.

But has Dever written anything that really let's us see what he truly believes? It's hard to locate, but here's what I found. One of the most consequential books of the last few decades posits that "racialism" really is what's dividing us. *Divided by Faith* by Smith and Emerson is the book that, along with Thabiti Anyabwile, shoved David Platt onto the T4G stage to criticize the crowd for being too "white." Well, Mark Dever wrote a review for *Divided By Faith*. He was just as impressed with the book as David Platt was.

Dever wrote this in review: "If you're reading this as a Caucasian-American, circumstances are not arranged for you to have to engage this issue. But if you're reading this as an African-

---

should be...American identity is inextricable from Christianity"; This is another one I found helpful; PJ Smith "usually supports a certain political party"; Andrew Whitehead and Samuel Perry "Taking America Back for God" a sociological study...They identified 4 different categories: rejectors, resisters, accommodators, ambassadors"; Tim Keller wrote a book review on this book "the more Christians engage in the Bible and prayer in community the less they move toward Christian nationalism...less likely to work hard for justice for the poor" Keller says "Christian nationalism is ... idolatrous... we'll be branded a Marxist"; Scottie Smith writes "the end of revelation should never be read we win"

[42] That division is along ideological lines, not racial ones. After all, Voddie Baucham, Darrell Harrison, Virgil Walker, and Samuel Sey are among our leading voices, and their skin is, well, dark enough to matter to those who embrace standpoint epistemology. Voddie, Darrell, Virgil, and Samuel don't think white supremacy is the problem.

American, you've never been given that choice. As our authors put it, 'Not having to know the details or extent of racialization is an advantage afforded to most white Americans.'" Count Mark Dever in the woke camp, because he advocates standpoint epistemology.

Next, let's consider Paul Miller, another writer that Greg Strand cites approvingly. Paul Miller serves with the ERLC, the wokest of all Southern Baptist entities. The ERLC is about as far left as Christianity Today. Greg Strand points out that Miller is writing a book with IVP on Christian nationalism. Intervarsity Press is squarely in the woke camp. Paul Miller positions himself as an expert who is able to speak against Christian nationalism, which is "the belief that the Christian nation…[is the] prescriptive program for what America should be…American identity is inextricable from Christianity." Heaven forbid.

Third, Greg Strand spent a great deal of his Christian nationalism presentation employing a construct invented by Andrew Whitehead and Samuel Perry. So if we want to understand the tree of Strand's presentation, we have to do a little digging to expose the roots of Perry and Whitehead.

Perry and Whitehead's book *Taking America Back for God* was a sociological study in which they identified four different categories of people relative to their views of America as a Christian nation: "Rejectors, Resisters, Accommodators, and Ambassadors." Strand doesn't tell us why he finds that arbitrary man-made construct helpful, but a little research into the teachings of Whitehead and Perry reveal that they themselves are rabid "Never Trumpers." Their original research was paltry. Their work was essentially a leftist political interpretation of studies done by others.

Samuel Sey offers a review of the book:

"If people like Francis Schaeffer and Wayne Grudem are Christian nationalists, then we need more Christian nationalists in evangelicalism today, not less. Since Christian nationalism is generally another word for a biblical worldview or conservative Christianity—I'm grateful it's more prevalent than critical race theory is in evangelicalism...However, *Taking America Back for God* suggests most evangelicals—including me and, probably you—are some of the most threatening people in our culture today. And yet, many professing Christians have become so undiscerning and so antagonistic with conservative Christians they choose to endorse and promote anti-Christian books like this."[43]

Strand says, "I don't like to classify, because then it's easy to condemn...the Ambassadors aren't going to be convinced but the Accommodators will be potentially." So Strand uses Perry's artificial classification system to decry classification systems.

In a Georgetown University interview about their book,[44] Perry displayed his Anti-Trump Derangement Syndrome and social justice worldview. "They're using Christian as a racial dog whistle." Christian nationalism "means our religious freedom to do what we want." Whitehead agrees and adds, "Christian nationalists oppose immigration and want everyone to look like them." But people who score high on their ridiculous Christian nationalism scorecard who

---

[43] Samuel Sey, https://slowtowrite.com/christian-nationalism-in-the-united-states/

[44] https://www.youtube.com/watch?v=OIV7k31pPtw

happen to be "P.O.C." (people of color) do so for a different reason. They "have an idealized vision of a Christian nation with tolerance and acceptance and kindness toward one's neighbor." So, Perry and Whitehead have invented a tool that serves them well in painting "white Christian nationalists" as racists and "P.O.C. Christian nationalists" as idealists. It's a wonder that anyone would take these political hacks seriously, but Strand built a major portion of his presentation upon their propaganda.

And if it appears I'm being too harsh on Strand, realize what Whitehead and Perry have been saying about our brothers in Christ. "The famous ambassadors like Robert Jeffress and Franklin Graham" were excited and liked it when Trump held the Bible outside the burned church. Tony Perkins, David Barton, they can very fluently speak the language of Christian devotion...but they are more interested in cultural and political power and influence." I am not attacking Stand. I listened to Strand shamelessly promote Perry and Whitehead, who are accusers of the brethren. To malign Jeffress, Graham, Perkins, and Barton, going so far as to say that their language of Christian devotion is a sham, is outright slander. Strand should be ashamed of himself for promoting Perry and Whitehead.

We don't need Anti-Trump Derangement Syndrome in evangelicalism. Perry and Whitehead interviewed 50 random people and called it research. They globbed onto a Baylor study of 1500 people and a University of Chicago study of 3000 to make it appear as if their book was data-driven rather than political. But all they did was impose their political commentary after choosing representatives to interview and to categorize as they pleased.

In the Georgetown interview, Perry tried to appear nuanced while accusing the brethren. "These are characteristic of fascist politics. I don't say 'you're a fascist.' But if it walks like a duck, talks like a duck. It sounds bad but when you read Jason Stanley's book and when you read our book; I don't know how you cannot make those connections. Electing strong man politicians, limiting freedom of speech and expression, no appreciation for diversity."

In this way, Perry presents Trump and his supporters as fascists. Whitehead and Perry's entire project is a leftist hit piece that has no place in evangelicalism. It is nothing more than Anti-Trump Derangement Syndrome trying to look scientific.

These are some of the men whose work Strand cited with approval, but what did Strand himself teach in his presentation? Strand taught that Christian nationalism has been brewing for a long time, with horrifying results. "You get the insurrection on January 6th." Strand thinks that what happened on January 6th was an "insurrection," but the fact remains that those who trespassed on federal property didn't have weapons! The fact remains that the only person shot at the Capitol was an unarmed woman. She was killed by an officer who has for some strange reason yet to be identified. To complicate the matter, video evidence proves that other police officers were allowing the trespassers to enter unresisted. Call it stupid. Call it nothing compared to the rioting that happened during the summer of 2020. But why does Strand call it an insurrection?

Even if he wants to call it an insurrection, which only plays into the hands of CNN and the like, where is Strand's evidence that what happened is in any way connected to the dreaded "Christian nationalism"? Strand laments the fact that in Washington D.C. on January 6th, "there were those carrying signs that said 'Jesus is my Savior.'" But why is that a bad thing? Would Strand please provide evidence against those sign-carriers that they did anything wrong? What are the names of the individuals and what sins or crimes did they commit? Which of the sign-carriers were among those guilty of trespassing? In a crowd of hundreds of thousands of people, there are bound to be some bad actors, but individualism is important. Every individual has the right to be judged based upon his own behavior and according to due process. But Strand is willing to throw the evangelists under the bus. Strand is going to great lengths to show that Christian nationalism is a major problem, something remotely comparable to leftism. But where is the actual evidence?

He laments the actions of Jake Yellowstone Angeli, that wolf guy who breached the chamber. Yet, Strand knows he is "a self-proclaimed shaman." So, when he prayed "thank you for this opportunity to fill this chamber…and…get rid of communist globalists," what does that have to do with Christian nationalism? This guy with horns was missing the Christian part, even if his nationalism somehow contributed to the problematic actions for which he is personally responsible. But if the guy with the horns was a shaman and not a Christian, why then does Strand cite him as evidence of the great problem of "Christian nationalism"?

Strand's presentation seemed more influenced by CNN than the Bible. When the leftist totalitarian governors gave executive orders commanding churches not to gather for the preaching and hearing of the Word (2 Timothy 4:2), not to gather for the celebration of the Lord's Supper (Luke 22:19), not to gather for singing hymns one to another (Ephesians 5:19), not to gather for the assembling of ourselves together (Hebrews 10:25), and not to gather for obedience to so many other explicit New Testament imperatives, we needed Greg Strand to exhort the pastors to obey God rather than men (Acts 5:29). Instead, we got the opposite.

Strand taught in his presentation with reference to COVID that "I don't have any rights. Yet how many times have we heard 'that's my rights'?" Strand decried the attitude in response to COVID lockdowns that "No government is gonna tell us what to do." The founders of this country, following Blackstone and Locke, understood that we have natural rights. These are inalienable, because they are given by our Creator.

Strand was intent to show that Christian nationalism is the great danger in the EFCA, but such an intention does not seem to derive from objective evidence. It appears rather to have come from a creeping postmodern influence upon Strand himself. Strand says, "The problem is when I conclude that every issue is a straight-line issue...we will speak too strongly...I affirm a hermeneutical spiral." The problem is Strand's nonlinear reasoning. He says in his presentation that "the axis of evil was used by one of our presidents," but what does that have to do with the price of tea in China? Where is Strand's evidence? Non-falsifiable assertions are meaningless and evidence that crumbles under cross-examination proves nothing (Proverbs 18:17). There was nothing compelling about Strand's case against so-called Christian nationalism.

My assertion is that leftism is the great danger to evangelicalism and that social justice is part and parcel of leftism. Strand's assertion is that Christian nationalism is a bigger problem than CRT in evangelicalism. He said, "This is an area where it's going to take more courage to speak about than critical theory...My sense in the EFCA...there is more Christian nationalism in our churches...You could speak strongly against CRT along with some of the benefits and get little pushback." Strand assumes there are some benefits to CRT, but he hasn't provided us with any. If pastors don't get pushback when speaking against CRT, which most do, that is because their congregations are discerning (Hebrews 5:14). Meanwhile, the examples Strand provides to substantiate the audacious claim that Christian nationalism is a bigger problem in our churches than CRT fail to accomplish the work for which they were sent.

In the same way that the left uses terms like "social justice, diversity, inclusion, and equity" to paint itself as being virtuous, the left uses the term "Christian nationalism" to color Christians as terrible people. For the life of me, I cannot figure out why Greg Strand seems intent to do the same.

"Christian nationalism" is meant to paint political activism coming from the right as a bigoted attempt to force our morality on others. Since the left sees morality as subjective, they have no concern that our morality actually is moral, over against their immorality. And since they champion immorality, they have no conscience about decrying our desire to impose our morals on others when they are every bit as politically active as anyone else. Both sides vote. Both seek to persuade others to vote their way. Both want to change the nation according to their desired direction. But for the Christian to do so is derided as "Christian nationalism."

Is Greg Strand right to join the chorus in decrying Christian nationalism? How should we think about Christianity as it relates to this nation? Consider the decline of Christianity in America.

Everyone seems to think that the "nones"[45]—the third of Americans who in recent years identify their "religious affiliation" as "none"—are rightly identifying themselves. The calculus many miss is that there is actually no such thing as irreligious people. "Nones" are unavoidably religious too. They aren't becoming irreligious. They are becoming religiously animated social justice warriors. Lacking a commitment to objective truth, they readily accept the illegitimate child of Marx and Rome. They buy into social justice religion, and make no mistake, social justice is a religion, complete with priests and activist congregations. But what happened to Biblical Christianity, which stands so diametrically opposed to social justice, and, one would have thought, should have killed social justice before it grew to adulthood?

The decline of Christianity in America did not begin 50 years ago. It began about the time the nation was founded. Much like the

---

[45] pewrearch.org "Why America's 'nones' don't identify with religion", August 8, 2018

devolution of humanity from our high point at the start in the Garden of Eden is the story of Christianity in America. Christianity in America was at its purest when the nation was born, and has been devolving ever since.

I hardly could have written anything more infuriating to social justicians than the sentence that precedes this one. Their hackles will go up immediately because in their worldview the *only* thing that needs to be said about Christianity at the founding of this country is that it allowed slavery. The social justice religionist is convinced that America remains a fundamentally racist nation today, and was even more racist back then. Understand that equality is the highest good in SJ-ism and you'll understand their fury.

But the SJ narrative is built upon lies. Christianity did not allow slavery. Christianity was, in fact, the driving force that destroyed the wicked institution. To use the fact that Christianity had not yet accomplished this work at this nation's founding as an indictment upon Christianity is anachronistic virtue signaling. The fact is, if today's social justice warrior had been a "white" American alive in 1776, they likely would have allowed for slavery. Is that because the Bible is pro-slavery? No, that's because the elimination of slavery is not the primary, or even close to primary, concern the Bible addresses. The Bible undermines slavery, and finally overturns it, but it does so by force of implication, not through imperatives. It is important to note we are all born in slavery to sin, and that is the biggest problem the Bible addresses.

Christianity did not introduce slavery to the world. Christianity came to a world in which slavery was built into almost every culture on earth. As Christianity went about its primary business of saving individual souls from eternal torment in the fires of hell and granting them eternal life, it has produced—in time—the side benefit of freeing slaves. Where Christianity has made little penetration into a culture, those are the cultures where slavery remains today.

Thomas Sowell[46] has shown that Europeans enslaved by Africans and Africans enslaved by Arabs outnumbered Africans enslaved by Europeans during the years of the transatlantic slave trade. Wherever Christianity goes, slavery goes away, case in point: America.

What made the Christianity of late 18th century America great—regardless of the social justicians' anachronistic virtue signaling against the very thing that has made America so free—has nothing to do with slavery. Early American Christianity was great because it was very God-centered, biblical, and moral—all of which have been steadily eroding since the earliest days of America's founding.

The founding of America is directly tied to the Great Awakening of 1740-1770. I could argue that the birth of this nation was *primarily* owed to the Great Awakening.[47] But suffice it to say that the preaching of George Whitefield to over 1 million Americans (80% of Americans attended at least one of the 18,000 sermons he preached

---

[46] Thomas Sowell, Discrimination and Disparities

[47] Historian Thomas S. Kidd noted that "the evangelical tradition supplied spiritual propulsion to the Patriot cause that was unsurpassed by any other element of Patriot ideology." (Thomas S. Kidd, God of Liberty: A Religious History of the American Revolution, p. 94)

between 1740 and 1770), the revivals attending the ministry of Jonathan Edwards during those years, and the great spiritual fires that can only be attributed to the Holy Spirit Himself during the years immediately preceding the birth of the nation shaped the people to be more God-centered, biblical, and moral than ever would be seen again throughout the development of this great nation.

Christianity's high point in the USA was at the country's very founding. Let's look at three ways Christianity has been eroding here ever since.

First, Christianity has been sliding away from God-centeredness. God-centeredness is an entire worldview that sees God as the reference point for everything. God is not seen as "a part of my life" or having to do with only "religious" things. God is seen as Creator of all. More than that, He is the Creator who never left His creation but sustains all things by the Word of His power. He is ruling the world as an absolute sovereign, providentially guiding whatever comes to pass. People are not the center. Humanists, please take note of that. People are made in the image of God, but we, like everything else, are merely created beings. All that exists, everything that happens with all that exists, is for God's glory. Everything exists for Him, and we hold Him as the reference point of our lives.

The Christians of 1776 were very God-centered. Since then, God-centeredness has been steadily declining in American Christianity. First Great Awakening Christians held Edwards' and Whitefield's God-centered theology, but the Second "Great" Awakening stripped that away. After one hundred years of Methodist camp meetings, Charles Finney's man-centered methods, and "restorationist" splintering (Stone-Campellites, Millerites, Seventh-Day Adventism, Mormonism, Jehovah's Witness-ism), God-centeredness was almost a vestige of the past. Since then, the downward slide into man-centered thinking has overtaken a vast majority of churches. By 1971, true God-centered theology was almost nowhere to be found in America, save the dusty old writings of men like Luther, Calvin, Owen, and the Puritans that founded America.

Amazingly, there has been a resurgence in God-centered theology over the last 20 years. Men like John MacArthur, R.C. Sproul, John Piper, Voddie Baucham, Alistair Begg, Greg Strand, Don Carson, Paul Tripp, David Platt, and JI Packer, although a mixture of friends and foes in the social justice controversy, have led a Calvinistic return to God-centeredness in this nation. Time will tell whether or not this will prove to be the beginning of a second truly-great awakening.

Second, Christianity has been sliding away from the Bible. Biblical literacy plummeted steadily from 1776 to 2000, as would be expected where there is a loss of God-centeredness, since the Bible itself and alone is what brings anyone to a high view of God. An average kid in 1776 could supply a questioner with 107 answers to a catechism like the Westminster Shorter. But by 2000, one would be hard pressed to find a kid who could answer the most elementary of biblical worldview questions, like "What is the chief end of man?". In the 1960s, Christians were still assembling by the tens of thousands to hear Billy Graham preach, but beyond that basic gospel message, knowledge of the Bible was a drop in the bucket compared to what used to be.

Third, Christianity has been sliding away from morality. Piety was naturally lost, following along the downgrade from God-centered theology to man-centeredness, from biblical literacy to illiteracy. Nevertheless, despite the man-centeredness of the Methodist camp meetings and Second "Great" Awakening meetings, they still stoked fires for the pious life. In the Nineteenth Century, America remained a very religious nation. People aimed for high moral values. But this was a two-edged sword. Piety without theology is top heavy. The moral imperatives of Scripture can only be obeyed by the one who has first seen and loved the indicatives. By the 1960's, the top-heavy religiosity of Americans was teetering. By the year 1969, the sexual revolution had toppled it.

Had you gone to a Billy Graham crusade in 1969, you would have assumed that Christianity was the dominant religion in America. Count people in the pews in churches across the land and it would surely look like Christianity was far and away the majority religion in America. Indeed, it boasted the largest numbers, by far, of any religion in the nation. Few would argue with those who called it a "Christian nation."

But by 1969, the foundations had been eroding for almost 200 years. The great falling away of subsequent generations whereby almost one third of Americans would call themselves "nones" (no religious affiliation) by 2019 was not only tragic, but inevitable.

Today, very few Roman Catholics or mainline Protestants are genuine Christians. The ones who are, and still remain in those corrupted denominations (praise God that the United Methodist Church avoided full-scale corruption with the Traditional Plan vote in February 2019), are far from God-centered, far from biblical, far from consistently *Christian*. They may have an outward form of piety, but they don't have the power that only genuine God-centered, biblical Christianity can supply.

The rise of Social Justice over the last 50 years should not surprise us at all, given the deterioration of Christianity in America that has continued unabated since the nation's founding. When all that remains is a shell of a living thing, we ought not be surprised when upcoming generations simply do away with the shell altogether. The rise of the "nones" was nothing more than the unmasking of a lot of unregenerate people.

In 2021, those who no longer claim to be Christian walk hand in hand with another third of Americans who still claim to be Christian but in no sense share in the faith of the nation's forefathers. These are "Christians" who hate any doctrine of grace that devalues their own human autonomy. The idea of a Sovereign God is one of the only things that is anathema to them. These are "Christians" who never read the Bible. Why would they? Their own human reasoning is all they need to form their opinions. And their postmodern definition of truth means whatever they think and feel is what's valid for them. Who needs the Bible if I already have "my truth"? And, of course, then, biblical standards of morality are dismissed as pietistic and puritanical.

It is right to call God-centered Biblical Christianity "puritanical," because the Puritans, by-and-large, had it right. Ever since the founding of this country, Christianity has been getting watered down. By 1969, a majority of what claimed to be Christian was apostate from the genuine. There just wasn't enough genuine Christianity left in America to resist the rise of social justice religion. Social justice has arisen as the dominant religion in America because so-called Christians have been drifting away from God-centeredness, the Bible, and Biblical morality ever since the nation's founding.

So, is Greg Strand right to join the chorus in decrying Christian nationalism? No, a goal of every Christian living in this nation should be to Make America Christian Again. Allow me to suggest that we ought to fight to recover what we've steadily been losing.

How should we think about Christianity as it relates to this nation? The decline of Christianity in America ought to wake Christians up from our apathy. We need to preach the Gospel in order that God would become the center of the worldview of more and more individuals. We ought to disciple these individuals in the content of the Bible.

And biblical morality ought to be the foundation of our political activism. Every issue the nation faces will have moral questions at the root. We must take a God-centered biblical view of morality into the public square to address these issues. The moral view of economics is contra Marx, contra big government, contra redistribution of wealth, contra social justice. The moral view of race, gender, sexuality, and nationality is likewise contra social justice. Free of wokeness, the Church needs to be the voice of morality to America. We are right to be both Christian and nationalist.

# CHAPTER 7

## NAMING NAMES

*"But don't name names or throw fellow Christians under the bus"*

Many who read *Woke-Free Church* will be far more concerned about this author's tone and the fact that I name names than they will be about social justice. Let God be the judge between us.

For my part, I believe I am learning from Jesus and the Apostles. Gentle Jesus, meek and mild, has another side when dealing with false teachers (Matthew 23) and worldliness (Revelation 6-19). What's more, the Apostles did not hold as a standard that Christians ought not call people out by name. If that were the standard, then how do we even know Alexander the Coppersmith (2 Timothy 4:14), Diotrephes (3 John 1:9), Demas (2 Timothy 4:10), and Euodia and Syntyche (Philippians 4:2-3)? We *only* know these folks because they got called out by name.[48]

---

[48] In addition to the Biblical examples, which are the standard, we can gain some insight from Church history. From the Apostle John with Cerinthus, Nicolaus with

In the case of Euodia and Syntyche, their names were exposed not for being overt false teachers, but for being disagreeable. Paul told his fellow yokefellow to *plead* with them. That is precisely what I am doing in *Woke-Free Church*. I am *pleading* with the men named in this book to correct course. Social justice ideology is highly disagreeable. It disturbs the peace. It falsely accuses the sheep. It beats the sheep for doing nothing wrong. It is a divisive Euodia-Syntyche spirit. Those who push social justice need to be directly told to stop, and if they have been teaching publicly, that rebuke also needs to be public (Galatians 2:11-21).

It is biblical and honors the truth to get specific. Speaking in broad generalities is effeminate. It makes it easy for others to use your words as ammo against people. The one who speaks out against "fundamentalists," but would never stand toe-to-toe with any actual person they have in mind when they speak against this broad category, is actually cowardly. To not name names when criticizing is far from charitable. If you are going to say something critical (and to be biblical we sometimes must), then be honest, open, and transparent about what you are actually saying and to whom you are referring.

In *Woke-Free Church*, I name a large number of social justice pushers. Now, to call someone a pushover is only marginally less flattering than to call someone a pusher. But the prospects for each are entirely different. The accusation of being a pushover elicits the

---

Arius, Luther with Tetzel, Calvin with Servetus, to any number of examples from the past, the great leaders of old were usually very direct. Even if they sometimes erred by being too aggressive, it is clear that our age has become way too passive, indirect, effeminate, and overly tolerant. It betrays a lack of concern for the Truth.

very response the one leveling it hopes to get. There's nothing like challenging someone's courage to get them to step up. But calling someone a pusher is usually coupled with the expectation that they will slink away. Pushers slink away because they do their work in the dark, and like cockroaches, they run from the light.

I don't think Greg Strand is a pusher. I think he's been pushed around by Tim Keller, Jarvis Williams, Eric Mason, Thabiti Anyabwile, Paul Tripp and pushers like them at outfits like The Gospel Coalition. When James White, John MacArthur, Voddie Baucham, Tom Ascol, Josh Buice and company published the Dallas Statement, the pushers of social justice didn't step up to debate. They refused to sign the Statement; then they slinked away. They trashed it when they thought the mics were off, but they refused to have the conversation when things were in the open.

Proverbs 18:17 and Acts 17:11 were evidently not a very high concern for them. Pushers have moved beyond willingness to debate and are now only interested in propagating that to which they are already whole-heartedly committed.

I suspect Greg Strand, on the other hand, is still straddling the fault line. The ground is shaking, and despite his earlier missteps, I expect him to land solidly on our side. The alternatives would be to overcome the social justice contras in open debate or slink away and become a pusher. I expect better things from him.

But remember how social justice became so prominent in evangelicalism today. Social justice rose in the vacuum created by the decline of God-centered, biblical, moral Christianity. So, many social justicians retain the veneer of being Christian, however man-centered, unbiblical, and immoral they may be. In other cases, genuine Christians imbibe elements of CRT without realizing what they are getting into.

Either way, the more you learn about what social justice is, the more you begin to spot it all over the church, even the so-called "evangelical" church. "Beth Moore pens a powerful letter about the importance of women leaders and the threat of misogyny in the church."[49] Russell Moore decries "the sins of white supremacy."[50] Whether Beth or Russell, it's more and more about the oppression of homosexuals, minorities, women, the poor, or immigrants by straight, white, male, rich citizens. The greatest danger of social justice is not what's coming at us from the outside, but what's coming from within.[51]

Christians in every generation face the threat posed by demonic ideology masquerading as Christian theology. It often takes far too long for Christians to recognize this when it is happening. The worldly philosophies of Marcion, Arius, Pelagius, Tetzel, and, more recently, Rob Bell were all welcomed in the church for a time, until valiant men like Iranaeus, Athanasius, Augustine, Luther, and Piper stood to confront them. Christians are peace-loving people, so we are not quick to make war. But there is "a time for war" (Ecclesiastes 3:8, Jude 3-4). Like Piper tweeting "Farewell Rob Bell," so there comes a

---

[49] Relevant Magazine, May 4, 2018

[50] russellmoore.com, March 29, 2018

[51] Enemies Within the Church,
https://www.youtube.com/watch?v=3zoe6tNmRyk

time for us to separate from those who cause divisions (Romans 16:17, Titus 3:10).

When worldliness threatens to take over the church, Christian pastors are obligated to fight that worldliness (Titus 1:9). Worldliness in the age of social justice does not simply mean to smoke, drink, or chew, or go with girls who do. Worldliness in the age of social justice means to say social justicey things. Virtue signaling is an example of acting worldly in this social justice age. We have to call those things out.

So let's focus on three social justice pushers who are currently masquerading as trustworthy teachers, and they seem to be getting away with it. I'll identify them by the fruit of their own lips, not by any unfair imputation of guilt. I cannot say for certain whether they are false brothers sent by Satan to destroy the Church or true brothers who have drifted unaware into aspects of worldly social justice philosophy yet themselves being saved. Either way, their teachings are extremely dangerous. So, without commenting on their salvation, and without meaning them any personal harm (I only mean to harm their social justice agenda), as a pastor whose responsibility it is to expose deceptive teaching (Titus 1:9), I warn about these men.

First, watch out for Dr. Eric Mason. Mason wrote the book that the title of my book addresses. "Woke Church" is an abject capitulation to the Critical Race Theory of the Cultural Marxists who dominate America's university system. Speaking at the MLK50 event[52] hosted by T4G in 2018, Eric Mason said that "white churches" need

---

[52] Eric Mason, 2018 T4G Conference
https://www.youtube.com/watch?v=TXF7WcLEwt4

to stop hiring token "black" people, because the only reason those "black" people would be available is if they were of too low quality for the "black church" to hire them. Furthermore, those who accept these positions are essentially Uncle Toms. In Mason's own words, "You have a person that's black on the outside but angloid on the inside."

Mason's type of reasoning is straight-up worldliness. He is bringing social justice into the Church. Whereas Colossians 3:11 presents a beautiful picture of unity in the body of Christ where "there is not Greek and Jew, circumcised and uncircumcised, barbarian, Scythian, slave, free, but Christ is all, and in all," Mason paints a world where the amount of melanin in people's skin categorizes them and prescribes the kind of behaviors that are fitting to their particular skin pigmentation.[53] It is social justice racism at its worst.

Second, watch out for Dr. Paul Tripp. Tripp has been learning at the feet of Mason ever since he began attending Philadelphia's Epiphany Fellowship, where Mason is the Senior Pastor. Sadly, the force of Mason's social justice wind has blown Tripp away from 30 years of sound gospel ministry.

It is Paul Tripp's own 30 years of gospel ministry that testify most strongly against him now! Every video series that has helped

---

[53] This is also what's so anti-Christian about the Enneagram. To pigeon-hole people by your perception of their personality and deal with them accordingly is the opposite of Biblical impartiality. The Bible teaches us to live by its prescriptions. We are to be conformed to the biblical pattern of what a Christian is, not get stuck where a personality profile places us. We are to relate to all people as the Bible commands, not as a pagan tool recommends.

families learn godliness, every seminar that has brought husband and wife into more perfect union, every child that has learned to honor his father and mother, and every father that has learned not to exasperate his children now stand to testify against Paul Tripp.

Paul Tripp said, "I am writing today, on the day following the 50th anniversary of the assassination of Martin Luther King Jr., because I have a humbling confession to make. For all of my passion for the gospel of Jesus Christ, which has been accurate and faithful to the best of my ability, the gospel that I have held so dear has been, in reality, a truncated and incomplete gospel."[54] Tripp went on to explain that the gospel of justification by faith is incomplete when not accompanied by the preaching of social "justice."

I wrote Tripp an open letter that was carried on several prominent blogs, posted on his Facebook page under the above article he posted, and sent snail mail to his office in Philadelphia. Others responded to Tripp's new teaching as well. To my knowledge, he never responded to any of us, and he has yet to retract his new-found theology.

Perhaps Tripp made this connection between justification and "justice" by listening to Tim Keller, who wrote the book "Generous Justice" and taught the same at The Gospel Coalition Conference[55] in 2014.

---

[54] Paul Tripp, https://www.paultripp.com/articles/.../my-confession-toward-a-more-balanced-gospel

[55] Tim Keller, TGC Conference, Sermon entitled "Generous Justice" https://www.youtube.com/watch?time_continue=4&v=280nS1_p2Kk

So, third, watch out for Dr. Timothy Keller. Keller is the biggest and the most subtle of all the social justicians in the ostensibly evangelical church in America. While books like *The Reason for God*, *Making Sense of God*, and *The Prodigal God* have marshaled widespread praise for Keller (which will no doubt turn many to scorn against me for opposing the scholar), Keller's ministry is infected with a toxin. The damage he is inflicting by his social justice pandering will, in time, come to outweigh the benefits of the good parts of his many books and sermons. Social justice is THE biggest threat to the unity of the Church and the progress of the Gospel in America.

I do not argue the point that Keller teaches many good things. But Dr. Timothy J. Keller himself says the following, "We must reweave society because it is falling apart because of individualism."[56]

And "social justice is giving people their due; It's biblical that we owe the poor as much of our money as we can possibly give away."[57]

And "In 1968, this was heady stuff. I was emotionally drawn to the social activism of the neo-Marxists...my hope is that all who read this book will become true revolutionaries and will go from here into churches that are devoted to actions of social justice."[58]

And "Just as the revolutionaries hide in the mountains, so Jesus Christ goes to the mountains: He is bringing about a revolution. He is a subversive. In the first verse of His sermon, He says, "I am

---

[56] Tim Keller, *Beyond Collaboration: Discovering the Communal Nature of Calling*

[57] Interview with Tim Keller, Christianity Today Dec 2010 on his best-selling book *Generous Justice*

[58] Tim Keller, *The Reason For God*, Penguin 2009

coming to bring a new administration. I'm coming to bring a kingdom, a new kingdom to replace the old kingdom."[59]

And "the new, fast-spreading, multiethnic Christianity in the cities is much more concerned about the poor and social justice than Republicans have been... I look forward to the vanguard of some major new religious, social and political arrangements. True worship must include serving the human community and caring for the created environment, doing restorative and redistributive justice wherever they can, building up the human community through deeds of justice, and being true revolutionaries who labor in expectation of a perfect world."[60]

Compiled together, the above quotes sound more like A.O.C. than an evangelical that most evangelicals regard as a trustworthy teacher. So, why do so many people trust Tim Keller's teaching? He makes many astute observations, offers a robust apologetic for the Christian faith, exegetes the Scriptures with dexterity, and frankly, is very smart.

But let's examine a famous sermon of his to demonstrate the error that most evangelicals are missing. In his 2014 Gospel Coalition conference sermon,[61] Dr. Keller's thesis is that "Justice is the sign that you've been justified by faith...A heart poured out in mercy and justice to the poor is the inevitable sign that you have been justified."

---

[59] Tim Keller, *Life in an Upside-Down Kingdom*

[60] Keller, Every Good Endeavor, 18, 19

[61] Tim Keller, TGC Conference, Sermon entitled "Generous Justice" https://www.youtube.com/watch?time_continue=4&v=280nS1_p2Kk

On the face of it, the thesis sounds pretty good. Who would argue with the fact that Christians need to live justly as the fruit (not the root) of our salvation? And to the great comfort of all true evangelicals, Keller stresses that he is talking about fruits of salvation, not works done to earn salvation from God. But subtle deception lies under the surface of what Keller is saying here. Continue on.

Keller says, "If you aren't intensely concerned for the quartet of the vulnerable: the widow, the orphan, the immigrant, and the poor, it's a sign that your heart is not right with God." That also sounds Christian. Faith without love and compassion for others and good works toward them is a dead faith. It is truly no real faith at all. We are saved by faith alone, not faith that forever stays alone. Good works inevitably follow faith.

But then Keller makes a subtle shift when he goes to apply his biblical exegesis. He is expounding on James 2, and he knows his Christian listeners are agreeing with his exegesis, but many of them are not ready for the subtle switch he makes at this point in the sermon. "Justification leads to justice. Justice is the sign of justification. It's like all through the Bible. Why would that be? A life of concern for the poor and doing justice for the vulnerable is the inevitable sign of justification."

Did you catch that phrase "doing justice"? It's still very subtle at this point. The sentence is agreeable on the surface. But Keller is actually beginning to conflate the categories of justice and compassion.[62] Should Christians have concern for the poor? Yes.

---

[62] People should not want justice from God. Justice would mean we spend eternity under His wrath. We should want mercy and compassion. In the Gospel, God is

Should we do justly in everything we do? Yes. But what does "doing justice" mean? Justice is giving people what they deserve, and the poor do not necessarily *deserve* the provision of their material needs. When we speak about providing for the poor out of compassion, it is dangerous to cast that provision as a kind of *justice*.

Notice at this point that the apostle James did not supply the word "justice" in James 2:18-26 at all. Now, it isn't wrong to use a different word than the Apostle when making applications of the Apostle's teaching. But that is not what Keller is doing by importing the word "justice." Rather, Keller substituted the concepts of compassion, mercy, benevolence, etc with the word "justice." The Bible supplied neither the word nor the concept at this particular point. It was a forked-tongued maneuver on Keller's part. When he makes his application, we see why he used this "doing justice" language.

Keller asks the question of what happens when someone who was spiritually poor but was justified by faith sees someone who is materially poor. "Are you going to say, hey, pull yourself up by the bootstraps? If Jesus had said that to you, you'd be in hell." Having already conflated the categories of compassion and justice, Keller now conflates the categories of spiritual poverty and material poverty.

Keller will admit to two separate categories of poverty. He discusses the spiritually poor and the materially poor when expounding the text of Scripture, and he distinguishes them

---

just in *not* giving us what we deserve because He gave our punishment to the Son.

accurately. But as soon as he moves to the application portion of his sermon, he collapses the categories.

Keller drives his actual point home, and it has nothing to do with what James was teaching. He says that Christians must not make a distinction between those who find themselves in poverty on account of their own choices and those who find themselves in poverty through no fault of their own. To do so, according to Keller, would be anti-gospel, since Jesus saw the whole fallen lot of Adam's race in our spiritual poverty and came to rescue many of us, even though everyone got here by our own doing. The final application of Keller's sermon is that "Generous Justice" is a gospel imperative to alleviate poverty at a societal level, not merely through private benevolence to those the individual Christian sees fit to help but through "doing justice" to the entire economic class of those who are materially poor.

Enter the world of Marxism.

This is a prime example of how Keller teaches his Marxist economics in the cloak of biblical exposition. The real teachers behind what Keller is saying do not include the Apostle James. Keller is teaching what he learned from Dorothy Sayers, Robert Bellah, Reinhold Niebuhr, Michael Schluter, and Vinoth Ramachandra—all Marxists whom Keller quotes extensively in his many books. He quotes them approvingly, not in order to refute them. But Keller's listeners just thought they heard a sermon on James!

In the sermon, Keller also glosses the fact that the good works described by James are placed within the sphere of the "brother or sister" (James 2:15), which is not humanity in general (John 8:44) but is a special attention to the household of the faith (Galatians 6:10). James mentions Rahab the prostitute. Her good work was not financial aid to "the quartet of the vulnerable." It was aiding and abetting 2 spies. Her works were "good" because Israel was on the side of the only One who is good (Matthew 19:17). The vulnerable city of Jericho was destined for God's wrath! No faithful application of James 2 would arrive at Keller's application.

I can do no better job of exposing the Marxist underpinnings of Keller's thought than was already done by Timothy F. Kauffman in an essay written for The Trinity Foundation. That essay, "Workers of the Church, Unite!: The Radical Marxist Foundation of Tim Keller's Social Gospel,"[63] is decisive at this point. Following Titus 3:10, Kauffman's prominent article was Keller's first warning.

Toni Brown's series of articles[64] is warning number two. Now, since Keller refuses to respond to these critics, I am saying that Christians should have nothing to do with Dr. Tim Keller. Brown was right to point out that the foundation of Keller's theology is faulty, beginning—like most heresies do—with a deficient view of sin. Brown writes, "Keller's misrepresentation and twisting of scripture is staggering...as he tells us that "disadvantaged blacks and minorities join gangs, commit crimes, use drugs and prostitute their bodies because they have no choice." Keller says "it's the obvious response to being oppressed." Nonsense. Scripture knows nothing of

---

[63] http://www.trinityfoundation.org/journal.php?id=301
[64] https://biblethumpingwingnut.com/tag/toni-s-brown/

such a claim, but instead attributes any and <u>all</u> sinful behavior to a corrupt heart that naturally gravitates toward, and loves the darkness (Jer. 17:9, John 3:19)."

Tim Keller is the biggest name of all the unnamed villains that Tom Ascol and company exposed with The Dallas Statement on Social Justice and the Gospel. When John MacArthur, James White, Voddie Baucham and more than 10,000 other Christians signed their names to the Statement, they repudiated Tim Keller, without naming names. But if false teachers are to be exposed, it is essential to name names. Timothy Kauffman and Toni Brown have done that, and I (along with many of the signers of the Statement) am willing to do so as well. We imitate the apostles John and Paul in so doing (2 Timothy 4:10-14, 3 John 1:9). Men like Eric Mason, Paul Tripp, and Tim Keller have name recognition (and "Doctor" in front of their name), but that doesn't exempt them from being called out. In fact, it increases the urgency to do so, lest many Christians fall victim to their teachings.

The battle against social justice is not just against those who are assaulting the church from the outside. It is also a battle against the purveyors of "the woke church."

The point in naming names is not to feel better about ourselves by knocking someone else down. The point is to protect the sheep from false teaching. "A little leaven leavens the whole lump" (Galatians 5:9). What's more, our sincere desire in opposing false teachers is that they would turn and be healed. For many years, we have been pleading with these men to change course. By private correspondence as well as public admonition,[65] we have reached out. Our aim in all of this is not to harm, but to heal. We are pleading with everyone named in *Woke-Free Church* to come to the table for an honest conversation.

---

[65] Sweet Social Justice, online teaching series, 2019

# CHAPTER 8

## CRT

*"But we haven't studied CRT, so we aren't into it"*

When accusations of Critical Race Theory are leveled against woke evangelicals, their response is often to claim that, until recently, they had barely heard of it. They never learned their views in the academy. It's just what they know by their own reasoning and experience. Are they being falsely accused?

First understand that *false accusations* make up the core of CRT. The "C" in the theory stands for "Critical," which is aptly named. James Lindsay was not wrong in underscoring this point by naming his book *Cynical Theories.* The essence of Critical Race Theory is a critical—even cynical—approach to life. It is to live like the accuser of the brethren (Revelation 12:10), constantly assuming the worst, always looking for opportunities to express grievance, quick to convict.

Greg Morse, a "black" man who writes for *Desiring God* did a tremendous job highlighting how false accusations function within Critical Race Theory.[66] I'll quote from him at length because there is so much value in what he has to say:

> After watching the George Floyd video and seeing the ensuing destruction to our city, the four walls of the house began to feel suffocating. I needed to go for a walk. I buckled my daughter in her stroller, and off my wife and I went. We discussed what we saw and pled with God on behalf of the Floyd family and our nation. On our way back, we turned the corner and happened upon an elderly white woman walking toward us on the sidewalk. As soon as she appeared to have seen us, we heard what we thought was a grunt of disgust, and she immediately crossed the street.
>
> What happened there? What transpired between that woman and my family? How we answer this question, as well as many others like it, I believe, indicates how successful the course of current conversations surrounding racial reconciliation will be.
>
> I could assume, as my flesh and the culture around me pressure me to assume, that she crossed because she saw my family's skin color. This coincides, of course, with the popular belief that racism is the most urgent problem facing men like me today. We live in a society deeply infected with racism, and thus, I should expect to experience racism even on a walk lamenting racial tensions in America. My experience was, in this view, just a mild form of what men like me face every day.
>
> Continuing with this interpretation, if I posted on Twitter how I couldn't even walk around the block without being racially profiled, avoided, and snarled at — while on a prayer walk with my family — I know people would grieve with me, denounce the racism of America, and retweet and comment about their standing with us. My testimony would serve as another combustible log for an already blazing cultural fire.

---

[66] Greg Morse, Desiring God, July 8, 2020 "Seeing the World in Black and White" (https://www.desiringgod.org/articles/seeing-the-world-in-black-and-white)

But as real as my initial frustration was, and as pure as sympathizers' comments and reshares might be, we would have conspired in an injustice against that little old lady. Further, it would have deepened in me (and others) a mindset that I am convinced enslaves those who hold to it. Let me explain, first, why we would have committed an injustice against her, and second (and more to my point), why I care to mention it at all.

First, to assume, and then to articulate, that she was acting out of a racist attitude is itself an injustice. Could she be racist? Absolutely. Is she racist? We — my wife and I, and now you — do not know, and it is against justice on our part to assume that she is.

Why should we suspend judgment? Because people cross streets for many reasons. She could have been robbed recently by a white man and wanted to protect herself against any young man. She could have wanted to avoid contact with anyone because of COVID. She could have abruptly realized she was traveling the wrong way. She could have become flustered at the thought of squeezing past us on the sidewalk (as we took up most of it with our stroller). She might not have even seen us before she crossed.

She could have walked by and greeted one hundred black men before this moment, but I — a six-foot-five male — could have made her uncomfortable. Heightism may have explained it. She could, if we knew anything about her, be married to a black man, have adopted African children, and have been a missionary in Ethiopia. All alternative possibilities. I could have misread the situation.

My point is that I don't know why she crossed the street. Her motives were not transparent. If she crosses with racial slander on her lips, making plain vile motives, the situation changes. But as it stood, I held only a vague suspicion — nothing more — that she did what she did because I looked a certain way. My impulse was to believe I could peer into her heart.

Greg Morse demonstrated that he is a mature Christian by curtailing any impulse to assume himself capable of reading the little old lady's heart. Critical Race Theory is the immature opposite of Greg Morse's approach. It allows itself to assume. It commends itself for condemning. It is an unrestrained accusatory spirit. It is suspicion run amok.

When woke evangelicals get accused of CRT, it is not like the pot calling the kettle "black." CRT majors in false accusation. To say that wokeness is CRT is not a false accusation; It is simply calling a spade "a spade." One word is simply synonymous with the other. It's not a false accusation to point that out. But lest anyone continue not knowing what CRT is, lest that ignorance become an excuse for being woke, let's consider what CRT actually is, because one doesn't have to fully understand it to imbibe elements of it.

Undergirding the popular discourse on the importance of being "woke" is an entire academic field called Critical Theory. As mentioned earlier, precursors to it began with Karl Marx.

The fundamental way to understand Marx is through Conflict Theory. Conflict Theory pitted the Bourgeoisie against the Proletariat in a zero-sum game. Economic resources were no longer viewed the biblical way, as the product of human work that man is commissioned to bring up from the ground (Genesis 2:15). There was no rising tide that lifts all ships. Rather, resources were viewed as a giant pie wherefrom to take a piece is to deprive a piece from someone else. Humanity is in perpetual conflict with one another, and more than that, there is an arbitrary dividing point that establishes two groups. The rich versus the poor. The "haves" versus the "have-nots." Marx viewed economics through this lens of Conflict Theory.

When Marxism failed in its first effort to overthrow the West, it refashioned itself in a more sophisticated and nuanced approach called The Frankfurt School. Over against the laissez-faire capitalism of the Austrian School, the Frankfurt School retained their Marxist goal but looked for "softer" means to bring it about.

The Frankfurt School was more patient than Marx and Engels. They were willing to wait for a gradual implementation of redistributive policies. As it would turn out, in the United States, F.D.R.'s New Deal, programs like Social Security, and L.B.J.'s Great Society programs would be found to be more socially acceptable steps in the Frankfurt School's "progressive" direction.

But the genius of the Frankfurt School was its recruitment of allies through non-economic persuasion. It took the Conflict Theory of Marx and Engels and stoked fires of discontent across society using various identity markers. It was first of all necessary that a person form the core of their identity in some place other than God. Whatever that identity, be it gay, female, black, brown, poor, fat, short, or whatever, recruiting them involved turning them critical.

The term Critical Theory came into vogue as early as the 1990's, but it is really not much more than Marx's Conflict Theory merged with the postmodern philosophical schools of the late Twentieth Century. Jacques Derrida of Duke University, and Michel Foucault before him, essentially took Kierkegaard's philosophy to the next level and abandoned any hope that objective reality was in any way attainable. Everything needed to be reduced to its situatedness. Claims to absolute truth are necessarily narcissistic. Knowledge is always privatized because no one can escape the panoply of circumstances and experiences and wiring that makes them think the way they do. Truth is a relative thing, not something outside of ourselves—corresponding to reality as it actually is—at least not in a way in which people would have access.

Well, this postmodern theory fit like a glove to the hand of the Conflict Theorist. Now, the privatized experiences of individuals could never be objectively questioned. If someone has a story of oppression to tell, if they have their own truth to share, then no one has a right to question it. To even attempt to falsify a story of victimization would be tantamount to victimizing them all over again. You would be imposing your Western worldview of absolute truth, your arrogant demand of facts, upon their all-important story.

When Thomas Sowell was asked by Dave Rubin why it was that he abandoned the Marxist philosophy of his youth, he paused and simply said, "Um, facts." Thomas Sowell had sat under the economic instruction of Milton Friedman, but even that didn't bring him out of Marxism. It was when Sowell went to work for the government and saw the inner workings of governmental welfare programs and the effect those programs were actually having on people that the facts convinced him of the folly. If Sowell had been a postmodernist, the facts of the matter wouldn't have mattered. But because of the common grace of God, Sowell still retained a Correspondence View of Truth, even as an angry young man.

Postmodernism gutted Western culture of that last bulwark against Marxism. When the Critical Theorists realized this, they merged the systems together. They began to push their ideology upon society through emotional stories, and whenever someone brought up the facts, they called them names—racist, homophobe, mansplainer, Christian nationalist.

Critical Theory intentionally seeks to turn various identities sour. The means is to get people to identify as a class of victims of society. The end is the original design of Marx's Conflict Theory, the people arising to overthrow society as we know it and introducing a socialist utopia in its place.

There's no disputing that the leftist academics are socialists seeking to overthrow Christian capitalistic Western society. Where people get hung up is the fact that most Americans have no understanding of Critical Theory, so, they assume, it must not be a very influential theory.

What that ignores is that the left is much better at telling emotional stories. Stories move people more than theories, let alone facts.

Critical Theorists don't put ads on TV promising to destroy the West, burn it down by revolution, and start again. That wouldn't fly with the majority of Americans who fancy themselves to live lives in the middle. Instead, they will paint anything right of the average American as being people who desire what they actually do desire.

Christian hegemony actually birthed freedom because it's not the desire of Christians to impose our religion by force. We are two-kingdom people. We live as sojourners in the city of man (1 Peter 2:11) as we await the city of God (Revelation 21-22), which Christ will bring from heaven after His re-appearing.

By contrast, Critical Theorists enjoy living off the capital of a highly Christianized society, namely the freedoms birthed by the First Great Awakening and the subsequent founding of a free Constitutional Republic with a Bill of Rights, but, ironically, they themselves are intent on imposing their religious worldview on everyone.

Critical worldview became the majority view in America over the last decade, but that 60% is driven by the 5% intelligentsia. The ivory-tower academics never came to Americans and put their views on the table. Instead, they practiced their theories. They told emotional stories, like the George Floyd incident, a story too rich not to exploit. They repeated emotional stories, again and again.

Critical Theory isn't academic in the true sense of the word. It carries the day in the Academy not by intellectual rigor, but by religious zeal. James Lindsey is a Mathematics Professor who set out to prove as much. He mastered the manipulative language of the left and then submitted outrageous and ridiculous articles to the Academy. He did nothing truly academic. He merely dressed up nonsense ideas in the language of Conflict Theory—grievance, victimization, oppression, marginalization. Time and again, the academics published his work, not knowing it was a hoax.

Critical Theory isn't an academic discipline, whose goal would be to dispassionately describe the way things are. Critical Theory seeks to change the way things are. It seeks to tear down and destroy everything that is hierarchical in society. The goal of "equity" is not an academic pursuit. It is a religious obsession.

That the evangelical pusher of Critical Social Justice doesn't know from whence it came is irrelevant to the facts of its origin. The evangelical that gets caught up in the story and the emotional sweep of the movement is responsible for offering support. If he offered it unwittingly, then repentance should come all the more readily, but don't expect it to come anytime soon from anybody but the humble Christian.

# CHAPTER 9

## DISPARITIES

*"But broad and obvious disparities of outcome must be caused by racism"*

An EFCA pastor and I discussed these matters at length. I used all my best anecdotes, from Thomas Sowell's conversion to capitalism to the following one about Walter Williams.

A young man approached the famed economist Walter Williams. The youngster felt safe approaching because the accomplished George Mason University professor had the same dark skin color as he had. It was the 1970's, not long after the systems of racism that oppressed "colored people" had been eliminated. No longer were certain water fountains reserved "for whites only." No longer were "people of color" relegated to the back of the bus. The Civil Rights movement of the 60's had ended such things, although the attitudes of the hearts of individuals could not be legislated. Individuals saw the world through the lenses of their own worldview.

Shaking the young man's hand, Walter Williams asked him what he wanted to be when he grew up. The young man said he wanted to be a pilot. The idea of soaring above the clouds in control of an awesome high-tech machine was thrilling to imagine. Walter Williams was delighted to hear his dream.

But then, as the crowd vied for Williams' attention, the boy made a comment as he moved along his way. He said something to this effect: "But I know I'll never be a pilot because the system of the white man will never let that happen."

Having heard the parting comment, after a brief distraction, Williams turned to see that the boy was gone. Contemplating what had happened, a sinking feeling in the pit of his stomach overtook him. It crept over him until it threatened to consume his entire body. He later described the feeling as "one of the saddest moments of [his] life."

Walter Williams lamented that he had been unable to tell the young man that it had been over 30 years since the Tuskegee Airmen, pilots with skin like theirs, flew their awesome high-tech machines in World War 2. The deceitful ideology that claims that the system of the white man would never let him fly was the only thing that could keep him on the ground. Crippling systemic racism wasn't even the case 30 years before the 1970s. Here we are 50 years after Walter Williams' soul-crushing encounter.

The pastor was listening. He was highly engaged. He understood that telling a kid that society is stacked against him can take the wind right out of his sails. Still the pastor seemed a little skeptical. Part of that skepticism was him trying to figure out my agenda. Why did this random pastor ask for this meeting? What's he really angling to get? What motivates him? The pastor was deciding whether or not he could trust me.

He trusted me enough to give me his time. As the meeting continued, since both of us were the types of pastors that are highly interested in culture and in trying to exegete not only the Word but also the world around us, we were both engrossed in the conversation. Before we knew it, more than three hours had passed. That's a significant chunk of time for a pastor's tightly packed schedule.

The pastor clearly recognized validity in what I was saying. And the volume of time we spent together indicated that I had established enough ethos to be worth his time. But something still didn't add up for him. Now he told me a story.

He said he used to live downtown. There was a family across the street that was constantly getting into trouble. They barely eked by, hardly ever knowing where their next meal would come from, always wondering if unpaid bills would result in the water being cut off, or perhaps eviction. There was constant drama in the house across the street.

But the pastor's family befriended them and one day they got invited inside the home. To their horror they saw padlocks on the outside of the kids' bedroom doors and learned that the parents would lock their kids away for bad behavior or when they got tired of seeing them.

The pastor's heart went out to the children who lived across the street. When considering his own children and the opportunities to succeed that were afforded to them and the disadvantages of the kids across the street, how can we not recognize that society is stacked against certain people? The system isn't equal. It isn't fair.

My answer went something like this. The idea that families advantage or disadvantage their children is precisely the argument that the right is making! The left's argument is that systemic racism is the problem. Our answer is that individuals are both the problem and solution. Individual sin is the problem. Individual salvation is the solution. Individualism, not collectivism, makes things better.

The pastor's anecdote would have been very different if systemic racism were the problem. In that world, good parents would be raising godly kids, but the cops would keep showing up to harass them. Racist laws on the books would allow officers to walk into houses and put "black" children, never "white" children, in their rooms and lock those rooms with padlocks.

The pastor's story illustrates that disparities of outcome can be traced to differences in parenting. The cops-with-padlocks story would illustrate that disparities of outcome can be traced to systemic racism. But the pastor's world is real and the other world is fictitious.

Nevertheless, objected the pastor, black parents still feel the need to give their kids "the talk." White parents don't feel the need to do that. How do you account for that?

The pastor was not a social justice warrior. He was simply a listener. A "black" man in his church had told him about how he felt the need to give his sixteen-year-old son "the talk." So what about "the talk"?

Whenever social justice warriors are pressed to provide examples of systemic racism in America today,[67] one of the first things they tend to bring up is "the talk." Because of white privilege, they say, whites don't even think to give their young teenage drivers "the talk" about being pulled over by police. Keep your hands at 10 and 2. Answer questions with no extra words. Say "yes sir" or "yes mam." And as Lebron would tell his son Bronny, remember, "we're literally hunted EVERYDAY/EVERYTIME we step foot outside the comfort of our homes!...#staywoke."

What broke Walter Williams' heart, and what never seems to occur to those who cite "the talk" as evidence of systemic racism in America, is that woke propaganda is a deceitful ideology that itself oppresses everyone who imbibes it. I can hardly think of anything more soul-crushing and detrimental that a parent could say to a child than that the world is out to get you. To train a child that they are victims, to instill in them a victim mentality, is the worst parenting move ever.

It would be like telling a child that there is a deadly virus lurking around every corner, that every passing person could very well pass that virus along and kill them. Such a warning would be fine if 1 in 10 kids were dying from the virus. But if the 43 states reporting show that "0.00%-0.03% of all child COVID-19 cases resulted in death,"[68] wouldn't it be child abuse to make a child paranoid about it?

---

[67] The burden of proof for establishing the charge of systemic racism is squarely on the shoulders of those who make the charge.

The idea that police are gunning down unarmed innocent "POC" is similarly a paranoid delusion. 973 people were shot and killed by police in 2019.[69] According to the Manhattan Institute, "As of the June 22 update, the Washington Post's database of fatal police shootings showed 14 unarmed black victims and 25 unarmed white victims in 2019."[70] Almost all of those 14 were justified killings, but even if all were not, when you consider that 47 million "blacks" live in America, there would be only a .00003% chance of dying this way. Compared to the 99.99997% chance of dying some other way, it is clearly a paranoid delusion, and outright child abuse, to teach your kids to be afraid of being hunted by police. "The talk" is evidence of nothing but bad parenting.

Thomas Sowell wrote a book entitled "Discrimination and Disparities." It is a must-read for anyone looking for the causes of differences in outcome. Jordan Peterson has done similar research, refuting cultural orthodoxy about the supposed "gender pay gap."[71] The big point to take away from Sowell and Peterson is that disparities of outcome are not *prima facie* evidence of discrimination.[72]

But there is a further point to be made. Teaching children to identify as victims is detrimental to them. "The talk" contributes to

---

[68] https://services.aap.org/en/pages/2019-novel-coronavirus-covid-19-infections/children-and-covid-19-state-level-data-report/

[69] https://www.washingtonpost.com/graphics/investigations/police-shootings-database/

[70] https://www.manhattan-institute.org/police-black-killings-homicide-rates-race-injustice

[71] https://www.youtube.com/watch?v=aMcjxSThD54

[72] In his book *White Guilt*, Shelby Steele of The Hoover Institute at Stanford University presents a compelling case for factors other than racism explaining disparities of outcome.

disparities. The parent who locks his child inside his room inflicts psychological damage that will go with him throughout life. Telling impressionable children that police are hunting them in the street does the same.

Disparities are a part of life, and if you want to find someone responsible, look in the mirror and look at God. God determines the times and boundaries of our habitations (Acts 17:26). Children born in America in the 21st Century have opportunities that were never seen anywhere on earth for thousands of years. But no matter when and where you are born, your parents probably have the biggest influence on shaping your life. Only you yourself have a bigger influence. Absentee fathers, regardless of their "race," have an enormous contribution to the disparities of outcome we observe. But even the parents you are given is determined by God. God never promised to make the world equal. He promised to save anyone who calls upon the name of His Son (Romans 10:13).

# CHAPTER 10

## POLITICS

*"But now you're getting too political."*

I mentioned that Michael Rice cited "white evangelical support for Donald Trump" as evidence of racism. Well, this raises an important question. Is the fault line beneath evangelicalism actually a political one?

I suspect it is largely that. But against the point of Strand's spokesman, Donald Trump is not the issue. Democrats would have painted as "racist" anyone the Republicans had put forward. The issue is whether or not voting for a Democrat can ever be a Christian option. One side of the fault line is so hot and bothered about having enough melanin out there in the pews and up there on the stage that protecting the lives of pre-born babies is optional. The other side of the fault line notices that killing babies is written right there in the Democratic Party Platform, alongside mutilating children, redistributing private property, and characterizing the Bible as hate speech. As a result, we say it is never a Christian option to vote for a Democrat. That's the woke and woke-free divide right there in a nutshell.

But how does race play into that? For our side, it doesn't. We're as colorblind as Lady Justice when it comes to moral questions like these. If the likes of Voddie Baucham and Samuel Sey had any less melanin, we wouldn't love them any more or less. We quote them because they speak the truth and speak it effectively. But the woke side misrepresents what we have always meant by "colorblindness." "Colorblind" was never a rejection of beauty in diversity. It was always an affirmation of transcendent morality. Martin Luther King Jr. rightly desired for his kids to be judged by the content of their character, not the color of their skin. That's what we do. Not so the woke.

The woke side of the fault line is very interested in demographics. Studying such things, they then shift their morality accordingly. For example, consider this Lifeway study[73] from a month before the 2020 election. "White churchgoers back Trump 59 percent to 30 percent, while African American churchgoers are solidly behind Biden (86% to 9%). The former vice president also has a sizeable—though smaller—lead among Hispanic churchgoers (58% to 36%) and churchgoers of other ethnicities (49% to 36%)." If saying that it is never OK to vote Democrat could result in the loss of 86% of the "African Americans" in the congregation, then the woke side reasons that morality must take a back seat to "diversity."

[73]https://www.christianitytoday.com/news/2020/september/evangelical-white-black-ethnic-vote-trump-biden-lifeway-sur.html

That so many "people of color" who claim to believe the Bible are willing to support the Democratic Party is what's dividing evangelicalism. Since Tim Keller is a registered Democrat, we know he thinks it's ok to support the Democratic Party. David Platt stands with him.

> "I look out in the church," Platt said, "and I see this person over here, who's sitting there and I know they are staunchly Democratic in the way they vote and work on political issues. And I look over next to them in the same row, and I see somebody who is staunchly Republican in the way they vote and the way they work on political issues. And I think, *That's the beauty of the gospel, when it has that kind of power, to bring together people who, otherwise, on many issues—many issues—would be on different sides of the aisle. But, when it comes to the gospel, they have a true unity.* I want that picture to be evident in the church."[74]

Half of evangelicalism thinks this way. The other half thinks they are out of bounds. Having strong Democrats in a local church is no more a picture of unity than having leaven in the lump (Galatians 5:9), wickedness in the assembly of the righteous, or darkness coexisting with the light (2 Corinthians 6:14).

In the 2020 election, a vote for Joe Biden was an affirmation of the things for which he stood. It was a murderous thing to do. The "doctor" who inserts the scalpel into the skull of a child in the womb of a woman is a murderer. The "mother" who brings her child, like an offering to Moloch, to that "doctor" to do the killing is herself a

---

[74] David Platt, The Gospel Coalition, Why David Platt and Ligon Duncan Repented of Racial Blindness, https://www.thegospelcoalition.org/article/david-platt-ligon-duncan-racial-blindness/

murderer. The politician who wields governmental power to confer upon a woman a "right" to kill her baby is a murderer. The voters who grant the politicians their power to invent and uphold the "right" of these murderers are themselves murderers. As we move down the ladder from intentionality and premeditation (in the case of the "doctor" and some of the "mothers" and some politicians) to the lesser intent of many voters, we may move from 1st degree murder to a lesser degree, but voting for murder is certainly some kind of murder.

Our side of the fault line draws a line at murder and warns those who cross it that they've gone out of bounds. The other side of the divide fails to recognize the special category of sin that murder occupies (Genesis 9, Matthew 23:35, John 8:44). So they excuse it. I don't know whether seeker-sensitive ambitions to never offend are involved in that. I don't know whether personal friendships make it too hard for them to draw a clear line. But it is abundantly clear that voting for Democrats is very near the center of our disagreement. It will be ground zero for the coming earthquake.

When I raised this point about a voter's culpability for murder when voting Democrat to a fellow EFCA pastor, he balked at the assertion. After further conversation, he granted the point. But he retorted that if it is never OK to vote for a Democrat, then it's never OK to vote Republican, because Republicans are guilty of comparable evil.

When I pressed the logic of the argument against Christians ever voting Democrat, he had to admit that it was never Ok, because murder is just that bad. But he still asserted that the same logic would make it never OK to vote for Republicans. When I asked him for examples, he cited war and the death penalty. But war is often commissioned by God (Book of Joshua, Romans 13:4) and so is the death penalty (Genesis 9:5-6). Noah's Covenant predated Abraham, so it was not particular to Israel. The fact of the matter is that the Republican Party Platform contains no comparable evil to the murder that is enshrined in the Democratic Party Platform.

A Christian is free to vote for Republicans or not vote for them, but Christian freedom becomes antinomianism wherever voting involves murder, and of babies no less. These children are made by God in His image (Psalm 139, Genesis 1:26-28). Protecting their lives is therefore non-negotiable.

Michael Rice, the pastor who testified on behalf of Greg Strand, said that "white evangelical support for Donald Trump" left black people feeling "skeptical," "scared," and "upset." Why is it that white evangelicals claim to "follow Christ, yet they seem to excuse things that are otherwise inexcusable?" Blacks can only assume racism. But such an assumption is the problem with Critical Race Theory.

Political machinations revolving around demographics are precisely the problem. Probably without recognizing it, those who have imbibed Critical Race Theory are identifying people by melanin and shifting their morality accordingly. If you accept that there is a such thing as a "P.O.C." over against "white" people, then you wear a lens that colors the way you view the world; It changes how you operate therein. Colossians 3:11 did not tell Lifeway to survey

135

churches, ask for their melanin count and which candidate they supported. Identity politics told them to do that.

But can we take this one step further? It is only the overly pietistic tradition of evangelicalism that prevents us from calling a spade "a spade" when it comes to politics. The word "politics" comes from the Greek *politikos*, from *polis* 'city.' Tradition says pastors ought not speak about the affairs of the city. But where stands that written in the Bible?

When the Nazi Party took control of Germany, pietistic pastors had little to say. When an equally murderous Democratic Party is taking control of America, pastors ought to reject traditional pietism that tells us to be quiet. The Nazis killed 6 million Jews. Hitler may not have done the killing himself, but the blood of the Jews was on his hands. Likewise, the Democrats and their policies are responsible for the killing of 60 million babies. Democrats have murdered 10 times as many babies as the Nazis killed Jews, and they are bloodthirsty for more.

Daniel Webster spoke at Plymouth to commemorate the 200th anniversary of the Pilgrims landing at Plymouth Rock. He said, "Whatever makes men good Christians, makes them good citizens."[75] That being the case, a political party is good only to the extent that their policies are good, and "good" is defined by the Bible.

Given the policies espoused in the 2020 election (200 years after Daniel Webster spoke at Plymouth and 400 years after the Pilgrims arrived at Plymouth), Christian support for Donald Trump was a no-

---

[75] A Discourse Delivered at Plymouth, December 22, 1820

brainer. There were two candidates. Kanye West didn't file in time to make the ballot in many states and I can't remember the names of the other obscure options that had no chance of winning. Trump supported life, liberty, and the pursuit of happiness. Biden supported murder, bondage, and the pursuit of Diversity-Inclusion-Equity.

The elephant in the room is that in 2020 the Republican Party was the only viable option that Christians had for casting a meaningful vote. Unless and until a more robustly Christian party forms, and the evangelical intelligentsia would decry that as "Christian nationalism," the Republican Party is the only thing standing in the way of a complete globalist Great Reset overtaking the government of the United States of America. I'm a card-carrying Republican, not because I think the party is doing everything right (They too spend way too much money and they too are full of swamp creatures), but because the other side of the aisle (There are literally only two sides of the aisle in Congress and the other branches of government are just as distinctly divided along the same lines) is openly advocating for abortion, mutilating children, Marxism, the Equality Act[76], no voter IDs, nanny state control, confiscating guns, cancelling businesses, controlling speech, and utterly trampling underfoot the natural rights that God granted to individuals when He made us in His image.

That's the state of affairs in the city. That's the political situation. The moral questions with which the nation is grappling are not

---

[76] Along with such absurdities as allowing men to compete in women's sports, the Equality Act would attempt to force Christian Schools to hire LGBTQIA+ teachers and would attempt to prevent pastors from preaching the whole counsel of God on these matters.

forbidden territory for Christians. Pastors have a special responsibility to answer moral questions, whether they arise in the private lives of individuals or as matters of public discourse.

The Bible has shown us what is right and what the Lord requires of us. To do justly, love mercy, and walk humbly with our God (Micah 6:8) includes pleading the cause of the oppressed, rescuing those taken away to the slaughter, and establishing justice on earth. We are, after all, the salt of the earth and the light of the world (Matthew 5:13-14). George Washington said in his Farewell Address in 1796, "Of all the Dispositions and habits which lead to political prosperity, religion and morality are indispensable supports." Only one of the two major parties agrees with Old George. Only one of the two major parties espouses principles that even remotely approximate the principles of the Bible.

Strand decried pastors and Christians who in the midst of a pandemic were objecting that the government ought not take away our ability to assemble for worship. John Dickinson defined an "inalienable right" from the Declaration of Independence as "A right which God gave to you and which no inferior power has a right to take away."

Michael Rice could only assume racism when evangelicals supported Donald Trump. But Trump took the side of freedom when Democratic Governors locked down certain states. Alexander Hamilton would have recognized the difference. He said, "Inalienable rights are not to be rummaged for among old parchments or musty records. They are written, as with a sunbeam, in the whole volume of human nature by the hand of Divinity itself and can never be erased or obscured by mortal power."

Tim Keller and Mark Dever are registered Democrats who receive nothing but praise from the EFCA powers that be. Keller and Dever chided pastors like John MacArthur for defying governors' orders to shut down churches. But John Adams would have stood side by side with John MacArthur. John Adams said that inalienable rights are "antecedent to all earthly governments—rights that cannot be repealed or restrained by human laws—rights derived from the great legislator of the Universe."

Democrats wield the power of government to steal, kill, and destroy. But Samuel Adams stressed, "First, a right to life; secondly, to liberty; thirdly, to property." He said, "Government...was originally designed for the preservation of unalienable rights."

Is the fault line within evangelicalism a political one? Of course it is. The Bible does not lack clarity when speaking to the moral questions that confront the city. 1 Corinthians 2:6-16 also promises that Christians have the Holy Spirit to lead us into all truth. We have the mind of Christ. We are therefore able to maintain Christian ethics and make ethical choices in the political realm.

# CONCLUSION

The way these controversies were settled in the good old days, before people got turned upside down (God put the head over the heart for a reason), was to assemble opposing sides at some kind of synod or council. Ideas were debated until the truth rose up over the lies.

Wouldn't the Free Church be perfectly situated to host such a thing? Why not invite Baucham, White, and MacArthur to sit in the same room as Platt, Mason, and Keller and actually hammer these issues out? Or if they won't (and the woke side won't), then why not invite the former, along with Jon Harris, AD Robles, JD Hall, Michael O'Fallon or any number of others who have been preaching openly against social justice? Why have these men been met in the EFCA with crickets? Why not platform those who speak openly and plainly? Unless the other side comes to the table and shows us where we're wrong (Proverbs 18:17), then what keeps the EFCA from becoming a woke-free association of churches?

The argument of *Woke-Free Church* advances five major points, corresponding to the first five chapters of the book. First, advocates of social justice distort the meaning of words in order to get the buy-in they could not procure by honest communication. Second, what pastors have actually accomplished, not the color of their skin, ought to grant them authority to speak. Third, social justice is the gravest danger the church is facing today, because it has a track record of shipwrecking faith and destroying civilizations. Fourth, social justice is an abjectly immoral approach to sexuality, race, gender, economics, and nationality, yet it masquerades as being virtuous. Fifth, social justice is a broad generalization of Karl Marx's Conflict Theory, the results of which speak for themselves in history.

The defense of the argument of *Woke-Free Church* answers five major objections, corresponding to the final five chapters of the book. First, the charge of "Christian nationalism" is often a canard that is meant to silence Christians in public spaces. Second, the real danger of social justice is significant enough that those who promote it within evangelicalism need to be openly and publicly confronted by name. Third, even those who deny being proponents of CRT need to answer for their wokeness. Fourth, disparities of outcome are not *prima facie* evidence of discrimination. Fifth, the politically-enabled atrocities of baby murder, child mutilation, and socialism, among other horrors, being promoted by the left through social justice language make it necessary for Christians to bring biblical truth into the realm of politics.

I'm asking the leadership of the EFCA to take a stand against wokeness. Whether or not they will, I have said my peace. And I encourage the reader, in your respective denomination, to do the same. Speak up. Toward that end, I offer some closing exhortations that I hope will help us to not be ashamed to speak out against social justice.

Wokeness is racism. Don't be scared of opposition or scared to look stupid for saying so. But turn the tides and get on offense, instead of constant defense. Christopher Rufo said it well.

> "No longer simply an academic matter, critical race theory has become a tool of political power. To borrow a phrase from the Marxist theoretician Antonio Gramsci, it is fast achieving cultural hegemony in America's public institutions. It is driving the vast machinery of the state and society. If we want to succeed in opposing it, we must address it personally and politically at every level.
>
> Critical race theorists must be confronted with and forced to speak to the facts. Do they support public schools separating first-graders into groups of "oppressors" and "oppressed"? Do they support mandatory curricula teaching that "all white people play a part in perpetuating systemic racism"? Do they support public schools instructing white parents to become "white traitors" and advocate for "white abolition"? Do they want those who work in government to be required to undergo this kind of reeducation? How about managers and workers in corporate America? How about the men and women in our military? How about every one of us?"[77]

Instead of trying to avoid being called racist, homophobic, misogynistic, nationalistic, etc, make the left answer for the absurdities they are actually promoting.

---

[77] Christopher Rufo The Courage of Our Convictions, https://www.city-journal.org/how-t-fight-critical-race-theory?wallit_nosession=1#.YILkBtW3blw.twitter

Be wholly committed to the truth and demand that questions of truth be answered. Truth comes before justice. Objective truth—not personal experience—is prerequisite to justice. No battle for justice can ever be fought until truth questions are answered first.

This is the fundamental weakness of the Social Justice "Warriors." They melt like snowflakes when someone presses upon them the underlying truth questions that must be answered *before* justice can be pursued. They have been taught that it is virtuous to crusade on behalf of "the oppressed" and "the marginalized," but they have not been taught to make a clear or compelling case that oppression and marginalization are actually happening. For them, it is enough to assume the case, so long as you are on the side of the ones you assume to be the victims. But every war to establish justice must be fought after a truth war. Once objective truthfulness has established the virtue of a cause, it's time to fight. Proving what's true must *always* come before justice can be established.

Commentators in the media have discredited themselves by crusading against accused people without due process. The *process* that is *due* to every accused person is the objective hearing of testimonies and all the actual facts surrounding a case. Without doing the hard work of uncovering truth first, justice crusaders are chasing windmills, wildly flailing their swords of so-called "justice." Social Justice Warriors need to learn that truth must always come before justice.

Don't worry about the charge of being "too political." Christians dread being too political by an arbitrary rule, but social religion is political by nature, so the fight isn't fair. There is no commandment against speaking to political matters. Political correctness is not a Christian rule.

"Theodore Dalrymple" chose that pen name because it "sounded suitably dyspeptic, that of a gouty old man looking out of the window of his London club, port in hand, lamenting the degenerating state of the world." He's an atheist, but that doesn't make him wrong about everything. He provided this invaluable insight:

> Political correctness is communist propaganda writ small. In my study of communist societies, I came to the conclusion that the purpose of communist propaganda was not to persuade or convince, nor to inform, but to humiliate and therefore, the less it corresponded to reality the better. When people are forced to remain silent when they are being told the most obvious lies, or even worse when they are forced to repeat the lies themselves; they lose once and for all their sense of probity. To assent to obvious lies is to co-operate with evil, and in some small way to become evil oneself. One's standing to resist anything is thus eroded, and even destroyed. A society of emasculated liars is easy to control. I think if you examine political correctness, it has the same effect and is intended to."

Dalrymple is right in his assessment that the Western world is degenerating; He's right that political correctness is like The Soviet Union's Department of Propaganda and Orwell's "Ministry of Truth." It aims to remake society by eroding morality through the shaming of anyone who speaks the truth.

I didn't expect to see the day here in America where Big Tech would so blatantly silence the speech of people they don't like, not to the degree we have been seeing. And the next step in the merger of Big Tech with Big Government that took place on January 20, 2021 doesn't bode well for the future of Free Speech in coming years. It is becoming increasingly difficult for people who simply want to tell the truth to be able to do so.

As Dalrymple observes, there is immense cultural pressure these days to do the opposite of tell the truth. Like mindless parrots (or worse...like immoral virtue signalers), we're supposed to repeat the most obvious lies: Men can be women. Women can be men. White supremacy is everywhere. Go to the Capitol "peacefully and patriotically" means riotously and violently. Impeachment is meant to bring the country together. Abortion is reproductive justice. Climate change is an existential threat. The Equality Act is loving. COVID grants government authority over a person's face. Church is nonessential. Some people's livelihood is essential while the livelihood of others is not. Dalrymple is right that political correctness is pushing lies.

But Dalrymple doesn't have the answer. Church, we do. Paul reminds young Timothy, "if I delay, you may know how one ought to behave in the household of God, which is the church of the living God, a pillar and buttress of the truth" (1 Timothy 3:15).

Here in the household of God, we have refuge from the world. More than that, the Church is a lampstand to the world. We uphold the very thing that is able to enlighten dark spaces! Since what God has made to stand will never be shaken, and we stand to uphold the Truth, we are the genuine ministry of truth.

Let's not lament like the dour Englishman across the pond. Let's redouble our efforts to proclaim the Truth to a culture that seeks to wield shame as a weapon against us. We have nothing of which to be ashamed. "For I am not ashamed of the gospel, for it is the power of God for salvation to everyone who believes..." (Romans 1:16).

I am praying for revival in America. I expect revival is coming soon, and I expect those who agree with the biblical principles espoused in this book to be at the forefront of it. Political correctness is only a threat to the degree that we retain capacity to be ashamed of the Truth.

There is a political threat to the Church. Consider the astute words of Dennis Prager, because having only the Old Testament, not the New, he still has enough of a moral compass to speak to the issues of our day. Silent churches should be ashamed that unbelievers like Dalrymple and Prager are speaking where they are silent. Let all Christians everywhere be set free to speak to these matters with such clarity.

"Socialism is this love of equality. So much evil has been done in the name of it. The idea is that everybody is equal, and not just in economics. For the left, everything is flattened out to equality. Parent and child are equal. The leftwing mindset does not want the parent to be unequal to their child, the teacher to be unequal to their student. Everything is equal. And of course, we are gods. We are equal. We are gods in our own eyes. Marx said it. Lennon and Engles said it. This is the beginning of leftism. 'I am my god. I don't answer to something higher than me.' A child doesn't answer to a parent. A student doesn't answer to a teacher. A human doesn't answer to God. It is a flattening out in the name of equality."

Socialism is a political threat to the Church. I know that Tertullian said, "The blood of the martyrs is the seed of the Church." Since even killing us cannot stop us, many Christians assume that politics has no bearing upon the progress of the gospel. It is true that even hard circumstances can result in gospel progress (Philippians 1:12), but does that really imply that the Church should stay within the lane of political correctness?

On the contrary, the greatness of our God to transcend politics does not relieve us of our charge to be salt and light in the political world (Matthew 5:13-14). We are commanded, "first of all," meaning this is a high priority, "that supplications, prayers, intercessions, and thanksgivings be made for all people, for kings and all who are in high positions, that we may lead a peaceful and quiet life, godly and dignified in every way" (1 Timothy 2:1-2). And if we must pray, are we not to work toward the same end?

The Pietists said we should *not* work for good political outcomes. They simply sang louder in their churches when Hitler's boxcars rumbled along with 6 million Jews in tow. But the political is not altogether separate from the spiritual.

When, in the 1950's, socialism won the day in North Korea and freedom won the day in South Korea, the "Jerusalem of the East," one of the largest Christian assemblies in Asia, was in Pyongyang, the capital of North Korea. Today, there are only scant traces of Christianity, perhaps 100,000 Christians, in the entire country of North Korea. By contrast, Christians in South Korea number in the tens of millions. It's fine to say with Tertullian that "the blood of the martyrs is the seed of the Church," but I think it is much more necessary to point out that, "Freedom is the seedbed of the Church."

America is the land of the free and the home of the brave. But ever since COVID appeared, we have been losing our freedoms at a very alarming rate. And it's not just happening here. All over the world, citizens are surrendering their rights to ever-growing governments. These governments, nation by nation, are themselves ceding more and more authority to global powers that be. The World Economic Forum promises a socialist utopia where people "own nothing but are happy" by the year 2030. The International Monetary Fund has designs to undermine the dollar. The United Nations is always up to no good.

I took a college course at the United Nations in Geneva in 1998, and even then, I could see that they stand opposed to many of the bedrock truths upon which the United States of America was founded. Their goal is worldwide socialism.

Revelation 17 describes the fall of a one-world religion. Revelation 18 describes the fall of a one-world government. The coming of the King in Revelation 19 will signal the end of all that is against Christ. But until He comes, the Church is the instrument God uses to restrain the rise of the Antichrist (2 Thess 2:7). The Antichrist will rise on the wings of Social Justice, signaling his virtue at every opportunity. False churches will be drawn to him. But for now, there still is faith on earth. There still remains a woke-free Church.

The time is now for free men to boldly speak out against wokeness in the Church. May God bring everyone who truly belongs to Him out of woke bondage and into the freedom of our King.

APPENDIX

## EXTENDED INTRODUCTION FOR THE EFCA

The *Evangelical Free Church of America*, like so many other conservative evangelical churches, is soon to decide between bondage and freedom. Will she be a Free Church version of Eric Mason's "Woke Church"? Or will she go free by the blood of the Lamb, in accordance with the gospel of grace, to walk in the liberty that was won for her at the cross? It must be one way or the other—captivity or liberty. Will the Free Church go woke or woke-free?

The EFCA has its roots in the pursuit of freedom. Centuries ago, the State-run Lutheran Church in the Scandinavian countries exerted domineering control over local churches. But the Free Church movement shattered those bonds. They submitted to no Lord over them but Christ alone. Their motto was "Where stands is written?," because the Bible, and the Bible alone, was their rule of faith.

But the EFCA, like so many other evangelical churches in America, has drifted from its roots in recent years. Many blue-state governors commanded churches not to meet, citing COVID as what supposedly gave them the right. But such lordship over the Church actually collides with the Lordship of Christ. He commands the Church to assemble (Hebrews 10:25). He commands pastors to preach, in season and out of season (2 Timothy 4:2). He commands the observance of the ordinances of baptism and the Lord's Supper (Matthew 28:19, 1 Corinthians 11:18). He commands we sing spiritual songs to Him and to one another (Ephesians 5:19). When God commands, evangelical churches need to obey, no matter what governors try to dictate (Acts 5:29). Sadly, the churches that understood these things and continued to meet during COVID were few and far between, and the leadership of denominations like the EFCA did not signal very much support for us.

As troubling as that was, this book is not about the bondage of local churches or denominations under the external powers of government. Government did not make the churches their slaves. It exposed our willingness to submit. COVID did not make the churches sick. It exposed that they already were.

This book is about worldliness *in* the churches. It isn't about the fence that the government built around Grace Life Church in Canada. That fence eventually fell, and even while it stood, the church found hidden locations in which to meet. This book is about chains in the pews and in the pulpits, especially in the pulpits. Social justice is a slave-chain that stretches right through the heart of thousands of local churches across America. Wokeness is a bondage that makes slaves of men. This is a call to be free.

Greg Strand is one of the leading theologians in the Evangelical Free Church of America (EFCA), and in my estimation the way he and President Kevin Kompelien respond to this moment will probably push the EFCA one way or the other. We're at that tipping point. And other denominations have leaders in a similar spot—for such a time as this.

Blame Voddie Baucham. In January 2019 I traveled to Atlanta for the G3 Conference and heard Voddie Baucham speak on the issue of social justice. That sermon—"Defining Social Justice"—can be found online[78] and is a helpful starting point for defining the terms of the conversation in which this book is engaged. Voddie Baucham has been speaking up for some time, but until now, few were listening.

In the spring of 2021, Voddie Baucham released *Fault Lines*, which has become the #1 best selling book in Amazon's Christian Ministry category.[79] By writing this book, Voddie Baucham has done the heavy lifting needed to bring us to a watershed. Since his book cannot be ignored, Dr. Baucham has put evangelical churches in a position where they have to flow one way or the other. Gone are the days when evangelical pastors could defer answering the questions set

---

[78] https://www.youtube.com/watch?v=YFNOP2IqwoY

[79] as of May 25, 2021 according to
https://www.amazon.com/gp/bestsellers/books/12360/ref=zg_b_bs_12360_1

before us. The slow bleed from the wound called "social justice" will either be stopped or the wound will be opened further, but pretending it doesn't exist is no longer an option. And this is where the healing begins. *Fault Lines* changed the outlook of the Church's war against social justice.

Now it's time to make a decision. Every pastor I know seems to recognize that the "fault line" is there. Whether they like it or not, they know that the people they pastor are wanting to hear which teaching they can trust. John MacArthur and David Platt aren't saying the same thing. James White and Tim Keller aren't seeing eye to eye, and we all know which of the two sides is willing to sit down and talk it out. The Voddie Bauchams of the evangelical world are always willing to have a Proverbs 18:17-style debate. The other side is not.

I've been a Free Church pastor for 5 years, just got ordained, and would love to pastor in the EFCA for the next 40 years. Such things depend on the way things go. And I think Greg Strand may be the difference maker for us. So I make no apologies about why I am writing. I want to win him over, and other leaders along with him. Moreover, I want every freeman to push as hard as we can to see each of our denominations go the right way. For me, that's the EFCA. For us, a lot depends on Greg Strand.

When my ordination thesis passed the Eastern district of the EFCA, it arrived in Minneapolis at the desk of Greg Strand, because he is the Executive Director of theology and credentialing. He serves on the Board of Ministerial Standing. The Board approved the paper, for which I was thankful. And true to his reputation, Greg Strand did more than rubber-stamp my work. He provided thorough and helpful feedback, along with encouraging words of exhortation. I have been sharpened by Greg Strand's input, and for that I am grateful.

In the Spring of 2021, Greg Strand addressed the pastors of the Eastern District of the EFCA via Zoom to warn us about the dangers of Critical Race Theory.[80] In his presentation, he spent an hour surveying the historical development of the theory and showing why it's bad. The presentation was thoroughly researched and helpful,[81] as would be expected based upon Greg's stellar body of work.

But then, in a sudden twist in the plot, he halted the word of exhortation and called upon a novice to carry the final 30 minutes of the presentation (1 Timothy 6:20). This man began his segment by admitting his lack of expertise on the subject, acknowledging that while even Greg does not claim to be an expert on the subject, he himself knows far less.

The "testimony" that followed was a 30-minute example of Critical Race Theory. The pastors were told that rooting out racism in the church was like a journey from Chicago to Los Angeles. From the 1960's to 2004, we made it as far as Denver. Most "whites" are content in Denver, because they celebrate the fact that we're no longer in Chicago, but most "blacks" are upset that we're not in LA.

---

[80] Greg Strand, Contemporary Critical Theory: A Biblically-grounded and Gospel-guided Response, EDA Theology Refresher, March 11, 2021, https://vimeo.com/user71521019

[81] There were, however, early warning signs in Greg's presentation that he is somewhat sympathetic to CRT, including a quote from Carl Ellis.

That's the status of the race conversation in America. We're at a stalemate because "whites" are too content and "blacks" are too discontent with how racist or not racist America is today. He went on to say that since 2004, we've progressed maybe as far as Carson City, but "there's still a long way to go."

Charging a group, or in this case an entire nation, with something so horrible as racism would require evidence.[82] So, this presenter asked the pastors to admit as evidence "white evangelical support for Donald Trump." This support, he says, left "black" people feeling "skeptical," "scared," and "upset." Why is it that "white" evangelicals claim to "follow Christ, yet they seem to excuse things that are otherwise inexcusable?" "Blacks" can only assume racism.

A second example was offered, but it actually didn't have anything whatsoever to do with race. He cited the grievance of homosexuals. They say that evangelicals are the "meanest" and the "most hateful" of all people. If that's how they see us, then we must be doing something wrong. Our approach "keeps them from seeing Christ." It is incumbent on us to change the way we're doing things and learn to "lead with love."

No more evidence was offered, but evangelicals continued to be charged with causing "systemic trauma, like racism, sexism, and all the —isms." We are hurting the "victims" and the "powerless." We treat people "unfavorably based on attributes they can't change." We approach people with "suspicion" if they aren't one of "us" but are

---

[82] The burden of proof, whenever an accusation is made, is upon the accuser.

part of the "them group." So we add to their "trauma" and worsen the "crisis."

"To think that we are all on an equal playing field now" is like forcing someone to run three laps of a four-lap race with leg shackles, then taking them off for the final lap and saying the race is now fair. "A majority of people will live and die never being able to catch up in a race that was rigged from the start."

That was his assessment of the problem. Notice the vocabulary: hateful, systemic, trauma, racism, sexism, victims, powerless. It is critical for every Christian to gain awareness of the theory from which this language springs. We'll start there in Chapter 1.

And what was his solution? We must "own our sins historically and currently." We need to repent. Then "prejudicial practices" must be "removed from our way of doing life" and must be "banished from our instincts."

But how? Well, Critical Race Theory "does indeed alert us to persisting problems that disadvantage by generations of supremacy." It can be a useful tool, even if not to be trusted on par with the Bible.[83]

The pastor giving the "testimony" actually recommended the very thing—Critical Race Theory—that Greg Strand set out to denounce. They went on to suggest we read some authors who can

---

[83] Article 9 of the SBC statement "On Critical Race Theory and Intersectionality" attempts to give some legitimacy to the use of CRT as a tool. "Critical race theory is a set of analytical tools that explain how race has and continues to function in society…these analytical tools can aid in evaluating a variety of human experiences" https://www.sbc.net/resource-library/resolutions/on-critical-race-theory-and-intersectionality/

help us along. Rebecca McLaughlin, Sam Alberry, and Thaddius Williams are among those who can help "alert us to corresponding structures of advantage."

We must learn "empathy," which is what the Bible means when it tells us to "weep with those who weep." It is especially important not to "blame the victim for the injury or assume they were to blame in any way." "Listen to people who are traumatized because irrespective of whether they ought to be traumatized, they are."

Now, one would have expected Greg Strand, who gathered the pastors to warn us against Critical Race Theory, to have interjected at this point and told us "you're on Candid Camera! This is classic CRT!" Perhaps this 30-minute interpolation was only one giant object lesson. I wish it were so.

Instead, when CRT was presented in living color, Strand said, "I just amen all that you shared." He said "amen" to blatant CRT after spending an hour telling the pastors why CRT is bad. Earlier, Strand cited James Lindsey's work as helpful to understanding CRT. But James Lindsey warns against "standpoint epistemology," which is essentially conferring special knowledge upon people based upon such things as "race." That is exactly what Strand did. He called upon a "black" man because he was "black." As this man himself noted, "There are very few people like me" in the EFCA, so Strand felt the need to elevate his voice.

Contra this idea of elevating "black" voices, Pastor Jordan Hall of Fellowship Baptist Church in Montana helpfully summarized the difference between how the world thinks about race and how Christians ought to think about race:

"Nazis: "Race matters."
White Supremacists: "Race matters."
Black Nationalists: "Race matters."
Critical Theorists: "Race matters."

Christians: "Race is a scientifically invalid Darwinian construct with no legitimate anthropological basis largely rooted in mythology, bigotry, and debunked genetic theories and is responsible for genocide, social unrest, and eugenics. Race neither exists nor matters.

We all go back to Adam and Eve, folks."

Christians should therefore be colorblind. That is why I don't even use the terms "black," "person of color," or "white" without quotation marks. The black-white binary is a man-made construct that explicitly denies the biblical teaching that all people are one race in Adam.

Following this biblical logic, there is no excuse for intentionally seeking to "elevate the voices of people of color" as CRT demands us to do. The people we elevate ought to have a proven track record of competence and a demonstrated ability to speak well to the issues at hand. We need a meritocracy.

The primary reason Strand gave this man—Michael Rice—one third of the time requested of all the pastors to hear about CRT was that his skin happened to have the requisite level of melanin to grant him authority to speak. Under the influence of CRT, what a "person of color" shares is sacrosanct, even if the "POC" completely espouses the very things you gathered the pastors to warn against.

I can guarantee that if James Lindsey, whom Strand recommended in his portion of the lecture, were to listen to the "testimony" of the "person of color," he would see it as a Trojan Horse.[84] Greg Strand then cited Jonathan Leeman and Tim Keller, who also have strong woke tendencies. If James Lindsay is someone that Strand recommends, then Strand should consult Lindsay regarding these recommendations. Lindsay has a strong understanding of Critical Race Theory, and he warns about those who are infiltrating evangelicalism in the Trojan Horse.

On the one hand, Strand claims to reject CRT, but on the other hand, he goes on to promote Carl Ellis, who speaks "from a non-dominant culture point of view." Strand promotes Ed Stetzer, D.A. Horton, and Pat Sawyer, who writes, "Critical Race Theory...has a place in my teaching, scholarship, and praxis." Sawyer says that he has learned from William "Duce" Branch[85] that CRT is better than white evangelicals at listening to stories of hurt. Notice that what was ostensibly a criticism of CRT has morphed into a criticism of "white evangelicals," because they say, "this is an indictment on the church, specifically white spaces in the church."

---

[84] Youtube, Sovereign Nations, The Trojan Horse - Ep. 1: Deconstructing Communities | Peter Boghossian, James Lindsay

[85] I have an old friendship with Branch. I even asked him to consider taking the Senior Pastor role at a church in St. Petersburg when the retiring pastor asked me to help find his replacement. If Strand and Sawyer are representing his position correctly, I would like to talk with him about it.

Strand affirms, "If you stay silent, the one who has a story of hurt gets further marginalized." Silence is violence. We need to "listen to people who are traumatized." Even though Strand denounces CRT as such, the category under which many of Strand's teachings belong is CRT-light.

I have no trauma granting me authority to speak, but speak I will, and do so on the authority of God's Word. From my standpoint over here in Berea, it looks like the leading theologian that the denomination has approved to speak against CRT is himself prone to it.

I don't believe Greg Strand is part of the woke intelligentsia. It's owed to the fact that Greg Strand helped to write one of the greatest documents in Christian history—the EFCA Statement of Faith—that I believe he stands to be helped. He clearly loves God and the Bible. I think Greg Strand is a beloved brother in Christ who has unwittingly imbibed elements of CRT, so I expect he will receive my straightforward public rebuke like Peter listened to Paul (Galatians 2:11). Proverbs 27:6 says, "Faithful are the wounds of a friend; profuse are the kisses of an enemy."

Because of the fundamental strength of the Free Church, I am free to write, without fear of reciprocity, concern for losing credentials, or anxiety about being punished in any way. We in the Free Church do not have the SBC's 11th Commandment (never criticize a fellow SBCer). We have "Where stands it written?" instead. So Strand won't show me the door the way Mohler booted Dr. Russell Fuller.[86] Free churchmen commend one another for being

161

Bereans. Besides, it obviously won't be objectionable to Strand that I am naming names because in Strand's presentation that I am here criticizing, Strand called out Eric Metaxas, Mike Pence, and several others by name.[87]

The book *Woke-Free Church* is a public rebuke to EFCA leadership for toying with wokeness, not realizing that wokeness is bondage. This book is a giant object lesson for those who can read all about Critical Theory but fail to see cases of it, or perhaps where they themselves have been falling for it.

Brothers, if this Greg Strand/Michael Rice presentation had been an isolated incident, I wouldn't have written. But this is, in fact, only the latest example within a series of incidents that make up a troubling trajectory that I've seen for years. It needs to be addressed.

For several years, our district conferences have had much to say about how we as EFCA pastors and leaders are too old, white, and male. For three years in a row, women preached to us in the main sessions of the EDA conference. First it was Jessica Cole, then Deb Hinkel, and finally Jenni Key, whose title was given as "Shepherd of Prayer and Mentor Advocate." Evidently, the leadership who presented her as such thought that "shepherd" would be more palatable than "pastor" even though the terms are synonyms. While Mrs. Key of Fullerton, California, preached to the Eastern District

---

[86] Dr. Russell Fuller was an O.T. Professor and one of the only signers of the Dallas Statement among the faculty at Southern Baptist Theological Seminary. He was fired shortly after he signed the statement and began to speak out against liberalism and social justice.

[87] Chapter 7 is devoted to the appropriateness of naming names under certain circumstances.

pastors, I opened my Bible and notebook and handwrote passages that deal with such things (1 Timothy 2, 1 Corinthians 11, 14, Titus 1:6, etc.), hoping to redeem the time. Without the chains of wokeness, all that time unduly allotted for Critical Social Justice concerns at our short annual gatherings would have been free. We could have spent it together on the Word of God and prayer.

At the national level, in 2018 Greg Strand introduced Jarvis Williams. Williams proceeded to dice up the body according to melanin count. In that sermon,[88] he commended "relentless antiracist work." He said gospel unity is hindered by those who "espouse vague pieties about colorblindness."

Jarvis Williams taught the EFCA that "every system, every structure and our churches…[were] built upon the backs of enslaved black people because their black skin was not white…We have to start here, because the gospel's not colorblind. As I've argued elsewhere, colorblindness actually perpetuates white supremacy and makes us apathetic and blind to racial injustices. This idea also denies the racialized experiences of black and brown people by suggesting to them that their racialized narratives are false, because they don't agree with the counter-narratives of majority white culture…Christian congregations that affirm colorblindness grossly fail the black and brown people that are in their communities…Antiracism, social justice, and reconciliation are gospel issues."

---

[88] https://go.efca.org/podcasts/episodes/episode-152-jarvis-williams-cross-and-racial-reconciliation?_ga=2.49051173.2095771600.1621950221-191177743.1621950221

Voddie Baucham deals directly with Jarvis Williams in *Fault Lines*. I'll submit the totality of his book and mine as my answer to the charges Williams levels against those of us who unequivocally espouse colorblindness in platforming speakers, "elevating voices," and treating others as we would want to be treated.

The EFCA may or may not be going woke. Who knows if most of the 1600 churches across America are drifting that way? But the Eastern District Conferences, the National Conferences, and the Strand-Rice presentation on CRT indicate that there are woke tendencies within EFCA leadership. *Woke-Free Church* speaks the truth in love to the leaders, and it calls everyone associated with the EFCA to reject woke bondage and walk in the liberty that Christ won for us at the cross.

Made in the USA
Middletown, DE
22 December 2021

56838919R00099